Church
School
Community

Lia McIntosh

CHURCH
SCHOOL
COMMUNITY

Forging Partnerships to
Change the World

 Abingdon Press
Nashville

CHURCH/SCHOOL/COMMUNITY:
FORGING PARTNERSHIPS TO CHANGE THE WORLD

Copyright © 2021 Abingdon Press

All rights reserved.

Library of Congress Control Number: 2021942003

ISBN: 978-1-7910-1896-2

21 22 23 24 25 26 27 28 29 30—10 9 8 7 6 5 4 3 2 1
MANUFACTURED IN THE UNITED STATES OF AMERICA

Contents

Partnering through the Seven Virtues of Kwanzaa

vii   Introduction

1   Chapter 1. Public Education in the US

9   Chapter 2. Partnering in Unity: Umoja (oo–MO–jah)

> *A practice of solidarity and embracing connectedness in family, community, nation, and world.*

19   Chapter 3. Partnering for Self-Determination: Kujichagulia (koo–gee–cha–goo–LEE–yah)

> *To define, name, create, and speak for one's self.*

29   Chapter 4. Partnering by Collective Work and Responsibility: Ujima (oo–GEE–mah)

> *To build and maintain our community together and make our brother's and sister's problems our problems and to solve them together.*

43   Chapter 5. Partnering through Cooperative Economics: Ujamaa (oo–JAH–mah)

> *To build and maintain stores, shops, and other businesses and to profit from them together.*

Contents

51 Chapter 6. Partnering for Purpose: Nia (nee–YAH)

A commitment to the collective vocation of building, developing and defending our community, its culture and history in order to add to . . . the good and beauty in the world.

59 Chapter 7. Partnering with Creativity: Kuumba (koo–OOM–bah)

To always do as much as we can, in the way we can, in order to leave our community more beautiful and beneficial than we inherited it.

71 Chapter 8. Partnering in Faith: Imani (ee–MAH–nee)

To believe with all our heart in God, our people, our parents, our teachers, our leaders, and the righteousness and victory of our struggle.

81 Conclusion: A Call to Advocacy

89 Partnership Actions You Can Take Now

95 About the Author

97 Notes

Introduction

On March 13, 2020, everything changed. It would be the last time that seemed normal for weeks, then months, and maybe years to come. The bell rang, and our kids left their schools for spring break, and did not return to finish their seventh-, fifth-, and first-grade school years. We never could have imagined that life would be changed so drastically over the course of a few days.

On March 16, the school district wrote, "After closely monitoring information from local health departments and government agencies, and after learning that the County has declared a state of emergency . . . we are actively preparing for virtual learning should these measures be necessary when we return from spring break."[1]

On April 9, Missouri Governor Mike Parson closed state schools for the remainder of the school year.

And Just So We NEVER Forget . . .

- Social distancing measures are mandated.
- Tape is placed on the floors at grocery stores to help distance shoppers six feet from one another.
- Nonessential stores and businesses are closed.
- Parks, trails, and entire cities seem locked up.
- Sports seasons are postponed.

- Concerts, tours, festivals, entertainment events—cancelled.

- Weddings, family celebrations, holiday gatherings—cancelled.

- Churches, synagogues, mosques—closed.

- No gatherings of fifty or more, then twenty or more, then no gatherings of ten or more.

- Don't socialize with anyone outside of your home.

- Shortages of masks, gowns, and gloves persist for front-line workers.

- Essential service workers are terrified but required to go to work.

- Medical field workers are afraid to go home to their families.

- Scarcities of ventilators for the critically ill endure.

- Panic buying sets in and we have limited toilet paper, disinfecting supplies, paper towels, and hand sanitizer. Shelves are bare.

- Nonessential travel is halted; borders are closed.

- A $2 trillion stimulus bill is passed, but barely makes a dent in an economy that is almost motionless.

- 1,185 people died of COVID-19 on the day this list was written.

This is the Novel Coronavirus (COVID-19) Pandemic, declared by the World Health Organization March 11, 2020.

I began writing this book shortly after the reality of a worldwide pandemic set in—after in-person classes had been canceled for the school year and work from home with sketchy internet and long Zoom meetings became the norm. We missed the social interaction of friends, coworkers, and teammates; we craved the daily energy derived from movement to and from work, school, and sports practices. Still, having a steady job, safe home, health insurance, and the privilege of working from home provided solace and much-needed rest from the chaos of life.

We mark this moment in history, because it is unique. There has never been an instance in our lifetime in which schools and churches are closed for in-person gathering. We have never known a community physically distant and unable to hug one another safely. The fear that grips us from an unknown virus is unlike anything we've encountered. Families, faith communities, and schools will be forever changed by the impact of COVID-19.

As a result, if there was ever an essential time to work together toward physical survival and safety, love and belonging, esteem and self-actualization, it is now. Abraham Maslow first introduced these elements and the concept of a hierarchy of needs in his 1943 paper "A Theory of Human Motivation" and his subsequent book *Motivation and Personality*.[2] This hierarchy reminds us that people are motivated to fulfill basic needs before moving on to other, more advanced needs such as spirituality. In a pandemic, our first responsibility is to ensure food and safe housing, health care and rest, jobs and education. This is the essential work of every institution, especially in times of crisis.

Likewise, this moment requires hope. Entire communities need something to believe in, aspire to, and rely upon. Although the immediate outlook of recovery from multiple pandemics is uncertain, we can still make the best of difficult situations with hope. In fact, hope is endemic in African and African American heritage and culture. It is exemplified in the virtues of Kwanzaa, which are unity, empowerment, collective work and responsibility, cooperative economics, purpose, creativity, and faith. These are principles that remind us, especially during crisis, that we're all in this together. Despite the diversity of ways we manage this unusual time, we have a shared humanity. At our best, we humbly acknowledge that we cannot thrive without one another.

A primary framework we will use to explore the foundational values of church, school, and community are the seven principles of Kwanzaa. Maulana Karenga created Kwanzaa in 1966 as a distinctively African American holiday.[3] A commemoration grown out of the ancient biblical first fruit harvest festivals, Kwanzaa celebrates God's abundance and the blessing of community. The seven principles or pillars of Kwanzaa are unity (umoja), self-determination (kujichagulia), collective work and responsibility (ujima), cooperative economics (ujamaa), purpose (nia), creativity (kuumba), and faith (imani).[4]

I discovered Kwanzaa while attending a historically Black church, St. James United Methodist Church in Kansas City, Missouri, led by Reverend (and US Congressman) Emanuel Cleaver II. As a newly married young woman separated from my family and the holiday traditions of my youth, I craved social connection and Black culture. The vibrancy of music, food, language, symbols, and teaching were a source of comfort and inspiration. I was intrigued by the year-end celebration that had been woven with the historical struggle of the US civil rights movement. The seven-day celebration urges communities to define and uplift themselves and one another. Each principle correlates to a specific day and symbol, to be celebrated annually from December 26 through January 1.

Today, we need Kwanzaa, not just as a celebration for African Americans to begin the new year, but as a foundation and framework for our ongoing communal life. Kwanzaa relates to the African word *ubuntu*. Ubuntu comes from the Zulu ethnic group in South Africa and describes the essence of being human.[5] It embodies community, interconnectedness, mutual respect, solidarity, and caring of humanity. Ubuntu serves as a spiritual foundation of many African and African American communities.[6]

I first encountered Ubuntu as part of my studies at Saint Paul School of Theology. I traveled to South Africa in January 2008 as an "immersion" experience with a group of seminary students. We spent two weeks living in the local culture and learning about history and modern society. Since ending apartheid and electing a new government in 1994, South Africa has undergone radical social change and multicultural transition. Its efforts at reconciliation and peacemaking, economic and faith development, have become an example for other countries to learn from in creating a transformed society.

South African professor Dirk J. Louw writes, "It [Ubuntu] both describes human being as 'being-with-others' and prescribes what 'being-with-others' should be all about."[7] In other words, being fully human is only possible when we are in relationship with a community of people, both believers and nonbelievers in Christ. Louw emphasizes that the context of ubuntu in African culture is both secular and religious and is a model of life and way of looking at the world. I believe ubuntu describes the essence of a healthy community, school, and church.

As institutions of faith and education, with a history of investing in people, the present and future of learning, growth, and health are inextricably connected. Church, school, and community partnerships are critical levers to help our communities heal and plan for a future where all students can achieve their full potential.

Indeed, the soul of America is at stake.

This book is for people who share the burden of leading into the future. You may be pastors or parents, teachers or philanthropists, administrators or executive directors. In all cases, we are curious about how to close the collective spiritual and opportunity gaps experienced between socioeconomic and racial groups across urban, suburban, and rural US communities. We are committed to amplifying the essential role of leadership in this moment.

This is a coaching book. It is not meant to be read cover to cover on a lazy afternoon and put away on a shelf. It's written to coach individuals and teams through the languishing educational, spiritual, and social disruptions our culture faces right now. It is filled with principles, narratives, and questions of resilience and transformation related to church, school, and community.

Use this book with your staff as a small group study, as the text for a course, or for individual professional development. At the end of each chapter, you'll find questions that are designed to help you see differently, analyze your context, and commit to new behaviors. It's hard to change the way we've always done things. It takes courage to admit that the old way of behaving is no longer working. It takes resilience to keep trying when the outcomes don't come easily. One of the laws of motion is that for every action there is a reaction (or resistance). To counter that resistance, Michael Stanier in his book titled *The Coaching Habit* reminds us to "start somewhere easy. Start small. Try to master one thing and get it 'in your bones.' And after that, move on to something else."[8] As we begin this journey consider using these three strategies to support your progress.

- **Set aside thirty minutes a day of quiet time to read and reflect.** During this time set aside your phone, email, and other distractions. Create a quiet place and space to read, pray, and journey through this book. Stop now, put it on your schedule, grab a cup of tea, and let's journey together. What time of each day will you set aside as reading time?

- **Invite a friend to journey with you.** During the writing of this book, I was reminded of the value of friendship. Friends provide a compassionate, secure, and trusted outlet to vent problems and frustrations and walk with you through conflict. My friends have been sisters and coaches, mentors and colleagues, paid and unpaid. Most of all they have simply been available to journey with me and remind me to keep going during challenging times. Who will journey with you?

- **Share what you're learning.** One of the best ways to retain and understand information is to share it with others and dialogue about its significance. Once per week create a social media post and dialogue online, chat with a friend, or intentionally teach a course. The journey toward partnership will sometimes be challenging, so intentionally infuse your journey with dialogue partners. Who will you share what you're learning with?

Admittedly, this book is deeply personal, sharing stories of my church, school, and cultural history. My practice of writing is a form of meditation and healing. When I am exploring through writing, I am asking God, the universe, spirit, to help bring clarity and to maintain hope in the midst of challenges. I have a dream that faith and education, inspiration and lived experience, can lead us forward as a community. I believe solutions to the world's biggest challenges can flow through prayer, writing, dialogue, and collective action.

This book will begin by expounding on the seven foundational principles of Kwanzaa for churches, schools, and communities. Throughout, we will apply these principles to partnerships with students, families, businesses, and organizations. Finally, we will explore a vision of citizenship and democracy to sustain communities as a practice of freedom.

Let's begin this journey together as an act of solidarity.

Chapter 1

Public Education in the US

As the daughter of an educator, reared in Christianity, I've never known a world without church and school. As a student, my learning journey began at a little private Christian school in the heart of north St. Louis, persisted through large public universities in Missouri, and has been enriched by experiences of mothering, pastoring, and organizing. My parents often reminded my brother and me that education was the one thing that could not be taken away. And while our educational access was wide compared to that of our parents, it still felt sometimes separate and unequal. Still, we were advised to study hard, follow the rules, and make the best of our educational opportunities. Today, we both have master's degrees. My brother is an elementary school principal. I am an advocate, coach, author, grant-maker, and minister.

Access to learning, growth, and education has long been an aspiration for my family, Black Americans, and all of humanity. Long before there were trained teachers, parents imparted knowledge to children, and communities taught life skills through shared traditions. Before there were school buildings, there were church houses with Sunday schools. Before there was aptitude testing, learning was demonstrated in daily lives. Natives, immigrants, and people from across the globe have embraced the process of learning and understood it to be as important as the knowledge gained. The steady and deliberate journey from inexperience to competence energized and built self-reliance. The thrill of learning new facts, beginning a new exploration, and mastering competency excited people—children and adults alike. Learning built confidence. Confidence enabled risk-taking. Risk-taking led to progress in humanity.

Over time, access to formal schooling came to be a symbol of unity and freedom, a perceived gateway to opportunity and respect despite one's race, class, or background. Education can lead to physical, economic, and spiritual emancipation. It's not just nice to have, it is essential. Without education, opportunities are limited, hope is diminished, and the actualization of one's full potential is stunted.

The first public schools in the thirteen colonies of America opened in the seventeenth century and did not focus only on academics such as math or reading. They also taught the values of unity of family, faith, and community. The Boston Latin School was the first official public school opened, in 1635.[1] To this day, it remains the nation's oldest public school. Public schools, or common schools, were community-funded institutions of education for all children of the region or neighborhood. These schools educated students of all ages, often in one room with one teacher. In many cases, local church clergy handled the responsibility for education in their community. With support from the community and wealthy philanthropists, clergy determined the curriculum, material, and teachers for common schools throughout the seventeenth and eighteenth centuries.[2]

Religion played an important role in developing an educational system in the United States. The Puritans, a strict fundamentalist Protestant sect who immigrated to America for economic and religious freedom beginning in 1609, believed that education was necessary in order to read the Bible to receive salvation. This was in line with the beliefs of the Protestant Reformers. Their schools made no distinction between religious and secular life and were also used to inspire children to endure the hardships of life through religious devotion. The first required education laws for some children in the North were passed in Massachusetts from 1642 through 1648. They were specifically oriented toward a segment of the population (non-Puritan) who was perceived as not providing their children with a proper education. Some religious leaders were concerned about the rapid growth of the non-Puritan population and took these steps to maintain Puritan religious beliefs. The first act, called the Massachusetts Act of 1642, made education a state responsibility. While public schools were not yet funded or required, education was, and all children were supposed to learn how to read and write or parents would risk loss of custody of their children. The law was amended and strengthened in 1648.

The law requiring the establishment of schools was passed in 1647. All towns of fifty or more households were required to form a school and pay a teacher either out of private or public monies. In addition, towns of one hundred or more households had to establish a secondary or Latin grammar school to prepare students to enter Harvard College.[3]

Fast-forward more than one hundred years. In 1779 Thomas Jefferson proposed a two-track educational system, with different tracks in his words for "the laboring and the learned." Scholarship would allow a very few of the laboring class to advance, Jefferson says, by "raking a few geniuses from the rubbish."[4] The upper classes were allowed to pursue an education beyond the basics and oftentimes attended Latin grammar or secondary schools where they learned Greek and Latin and studied the classics in preparation for a college education.[5] This normalized the classism and elitism that divides, not unifies or expands, educational opportunities for all students.

By the mid-1800s, academics became the sole responsibility of public schools as a means to assimilate children into the American ruling class's way of life.[6] In the southern US, "public schools were not common during the 1600s and the early 1700s. Affluent families paid private tutors to educate their children. . . . Public schooling in the South was not widespread until the Reconstruction Era after the American Civil War."[7]

By 1900, thirty-one states had required school attendance for students from ages eight through fourteen. "By 1918, every state required students to complete elementary school. . . . The idea of a progressive education, educating the child to reach his full potential and actively promoting and participating in a democratic society, began in the late 1800s and became widespread by the 1930s."[8] John Dewey, famous for the decimal system named after him, wrote, "To prepare him for the future life means to give him command of himself; it means to train him that he will have the full and ready use of all his capacities."[9]

Almost one hundred years after the United States abolished slavery, through the 1960s, Black Americans continued to be marginalized through enforced segregation and diminished access to everything from housing and public parks, to restaurants and swimming pools, even cemeteries and jails. This included a racially segregated system of public schools upheld years beyond the 1954 *Brown v. Board of Education* Supreme Court ruling. The aspiration of a democratized education describes the desire of parents and students, yesterday and today.

W. E. B. Du Bois, Black American professor of history, sociology, and economics at Atlanta University and one of the founders of the National Association for the Advancement of Colored People (NAACP), wrote in the early twentieth century, "Education and work are the levers to uplift a people. Work alone will not do it unless inspired by the right ideals and guided by intelligence. Education must not simply teach work—it must teach Life."[10]

By the late 1970s, legally segregated schooling based on race in the United States was eliminated. But a 2020 *New York Times* article described the reality: "More than half of the nation's schoolchildren are in racially concentrated districts, where over 75 percent of students are either white or nonwhite." School districts are often segregated by income. The interconnection of racial and economic segregation has increased educational gaps between rich and poor students, and between white students and students of color.[11] School segregation and educational inequity are often uncomfortable topics for students and teachers, clergy and business leaders. Nevertheless, this is an essential conversation. The consequences of segregation and inequity affect every American, one way or another. Our reality stands in harsh contrast with the core American ideals of equality and fairness, upon which our churches, schools, and civic leadership claim to be built. Until education is no longer separate or unequal, we have an abundance of work to do.[12]

So where do we go from here? How do we practice solidarity and embrace connectedness in family, community, and nation? School, church, and community leaders might understandably wonder where to begin, or how to gain even a basic understanding of the inequities in their community. But this is the first step: we must see and understand what is happening in our own towns, cities, and neighborhoods.

Historical insight and national trends can provide a helpful starting point and frame of reference. Research points to persistent racial, economic, and gender gaps in educational achievement across the country. Essentially, we have a caste system of haves and have-nots. This system exists across the US with much similarity from place to place. For example, in 2019 the National Association of Educational Progress (NAEP) reported growing disparities between the nation's highest and lowest achievers in math and reading between 2009 and 2019.[13] This pattern holds true across states and across student groups by race/ethnicity and socioeconomic status.

From here, start by asking, Do the conditions in your church, school, or community mirror national trends? I'd predict that the data may be the same.

Main Points to Remember

- A practice of solidarity is embracing connectedness in family and community.

- Despite a history of enslavement, access to learning, growth, and education has long been an aspiration for Black Americans, and all of humanity.

- Religion played an important role in developing an educational system in the United States.

- "Education and work are the levers to uplift a people. Work alone will not do it unless inspired by the right ideals and guided by intelligence. Education must not simply teach work—it must teach Life."[14]

- School segregation and educational inequity are often uncomfortable topics for students and teachers, clergy and business leaders. Nevertheless, this is an essential conversation. The consequences of segregation and inequity affect every American, one way or another.

Questions for Discussion and Action

As we continue this journey toward unity, consider the following historical questions to discuss with your team, neighbors, or group of concerned citizens.

What's the history of education in your community? Who can you talk with to better understand this history?

How has the population of school-aged children grown or declined?

How has the demographic makeup of school-aged children shifted over time?

How has the demographic makeup of teachers and leaders shifted over time?

Which students have thrived academically? Who's struggled? Why?

Chapter 2

Partnering in Unity

Umoja (oo–MO–jah)

A practice of solidarity and embracing
connectedness in family, community,
nation, and world.

While there is no single agreed-upon understanding of unity, the
following definition, adapted from the United Nations, is one I find
inspiring. The definition and goal of social inclusion is to create "a more
stable, safe and just society for all, in which every individual, each with
rights and responsibilities, has an active role to play. Such an inclusive
society must be based on the principles of embracing—not coercing or
forcing—diversity and using participatory processes that involve all
stakeholders in the decision-making that affects their lives."[1] In short,
unity is not about "I," it is "we." Unless we are all well, none of us is well.

Partnering with School and Community Leaders

The year was 1861 and Hickman's Mill in south Kansas City, Missouri, was a business started by settlers and served as a landmark in the woods. Leading up to and during Civil War battles between Missouri and Kansas, it served as a place of shelter and assistance for the Confederate Army. Missouri was a pro-slavery state.

In December 1861, the newspapers reported, "We learn that Jennison made a little excursion into the rebel country, from Kansas City, and burned Hickman's Mills together with three or four houses of notorious rebels at Independence."[2] The Union Army took hold of Hickman's Mill. After the war, Hickman's Mill was abandoned, and some families reluctantly returned to their destroyed land to try to piece their lives back together. "Until the 1950s, Hickman Mills was described as a 'quiet, peaceful roadside village.' Then, housing development engulfed much of the original charm as Ruskin Heights tract housing was built."[3]

Rapid housing and road development, due to the GI bill and other government programs post–World War II, enabled suburbanization and population growth within the Hickman Mills school district boundaries. It is located approximately ten miles from downtown Kansas City. White families moved to the area and sent their children to school. Black families were not permitted to live in Hickman Mills due to racial covenants and redlining.

As detailed by Aaron Tyler Rife in his dissertation, "Shifting Identities in South Kansas City: Hickman Mills's Transformation from a Suburban to Urban School District," he writes that historically, Hickman Mills was the state's first consolidated school district. It originally was all-white but has since become predominantly black with many households who are experiencing poverty. While it held an early "A" rating from the Missouri Board of Education, today it struggles to maintain accreditation and academic excellence.[4]

My personal relationship with the Hickman Mills School District began with my husband's stories of his high school experiences. He was a proud graduate of Hickman Mills High School, home of the Cougars! I came to appreciate its history and long for its former vibrancy.

As a pastor newly graduated from seminary in my first full-time appointment, I prepared to plant Renaissance United Methodist Church in the Hickman Mills School District. The launch team and I met and quickly established relationships with the superintendent, administration, and staff. We learned the school's mission was aligned with our mission as a church. The ethnic diversity in the schools reflected that of the community, as did our church, with enrollment being 69 percent African American, 13 percent Hispanic, 9 percent white, and 3 percent other.

Today, the mission of the Hickman Mills C-1 School District, a proudly diverse and historic community, is to provide a foundation for students that maximizes academic success and fosters civic engagement, as distinguished by:

- highly effective teaching focused on rigor and individual student needs;

- building strong family, community, and school partnerships;

- collaborative and data-driven decision making;

- the integration of technology across the curriculum and the district; and

- commitment to early childhood and ongoing college and/or career preparation.[5]

The Hickman Mills School District was Renaissance Church's first, and most vibrant, church/community partner. I went on to pastor St. Luke's United Methodist Church and continued to partner with schools within Hickman Mills. Today, partnerships with faith communities remain vital to the school district, with faith communities partnering to host virtual learning, mentor students, beautify buildings, host summer camps, serve Thanksgiving dinner, provide school uniforms, donate hats and gloves, host teacher appreciation events, and more.

While these are worthy ways to serve one's community and address immediate needs, I always wondered why just a few miles away, more white and affluent districts did not face the same practical or academic achievement challenges. I wondered what caused some families to linger in poverty with insecure housing while half-million-dollar homes were being built just a few miles away. What is the origin of these inequities and the resulting "achievement gap"?

In my reflection on the history, I discovered five distinct challenges within the community and school district, between 1957 and 2000, that significantly shifted district and community identity and outcomes. The challenges include:

- natural disaster causing death and destruction,
- a desire for independence,
- white flight,
- opposition to affordable housing,
- and perception as an "unsafe" place.

First, on May 20, 1957, a tornado hit the Hickman Mills area in south Kansas City, destroying Ruskin High School, Ruskin Junior High, and part of C. A. Burke Elementary, along with homes and businesses. Forty-eight people died, and over five hundred were injured. After the destruction, the community came together to repair and reconstruct homes, schools, and businesses with the hope of rebuilding the community.[6]

Second, this was a community that wished to remain independent but found the economic costs to be self-sufficient were too high. "The change from being a small but growing suburb south of Kansas City to being a part of the larger municipality, the community's refusal to join the Kansas City Missouri School District, and serious funding issues and tax battles laid the foundation for the eventual decline of Hickman Mills as a school district."[7]

Third, Hickman Mills, almost an exclusively white area, began to publicly address integration when confronted with the perceived threat of joining the Kansas City Missouri School District in 1964. Over the next three decades African Americans migrated south of the city for newer housing, economic development, and schools just as whites had done in the 1950s and 1960s. By the 1980s and 1990s many whites became nervous about property values, neighborhood "safety," and school quality, causing white flight farther to the south, east, and north to places such as Lee's Summit, Raymore, Peculiar, Independence, and Liberty.[8]

Fourth, a long-standing conflict between Hickman Mills neighborhoods and the Kansas City Housing and Urban Development (HUD) office existed. HUD officials worked to provide affordable housing for people who wanted to live in the Hickman Mills area. In particular, the Housing Authority of Kansas City (HAKC), which worked in conjunction with HUD, was under pressure to build affordable housing in suburban areas so as not to continue concentrating Black families in closed neighborhoods as the city had been doing in the past. Most of Hickman Mills neighborhoods opposed the building of affordable housing until the late 1980s.[9]

Finally, by the end of the 1990s, the challenges Hickman Mills C-1 School District faced were results of economic decline resulting from an exodus of long-time residents. Its conversion from a rural to suburban to urban community, as well as the perception of the school district changing from "good" to "bad," correlates to the increase of racial minorities, especially Black residents and students. Aaron Rife argues in his research, that "the change Hickman Mills underwent was largely a result of how its neighborhoods were perceived as racial spaces, first as white and 'normal,' then as Black and 'unsafe.' Ultimately, this study exemplifies how the social construction of space plays a significant role in neighborhoods and schools."[10]

So, what does this mean for church, school, and community partnerships today? How do we foster unity with school and community members despite the sometimes calamitous history of a community? Here are five steps.

1. Learn the history of your community.

2. Build relationships with community leaders.

3. Identify community assets and challenges.

4. Understand underlying systemic causes of problems.

5. Co-develop immediate and longer-term systemic solutions.

While we won't go into depth on each step here, learning the history, building relationships and understanding systemic causes are essential.

In every community there are "people of peace" who welcome new people and extend radical hospitality. They are people who are trusted, known, and have often lived in the community for years. They are open to new ideas and easily build trust. As the relationship grows this person opens the door to more people in the community hearing and being responsive to leveraging community strengths and solving problems collaboratively.[11]

Persons of Peace can be tremendously helpful in understanding systemic issues. A person of peace introduced me to the Racial Equity Institute (REI)'s groundwater approach to understanding racial inclusion and diversity. Here's an excerpt of the approach.

> The fish, the lake and the groundwater: If you have a lake in front of your house and one fish is floating belly-up dead, it makes sense to analyze the fish. What is wrong with it? Imagine the fish is one student failing in the education system. We'd ask: did it study hard enough? Is it

getting the support it needs at home? But if you come out to that same lake and half the fish are floating belly-up dead, what should you do? This time you've got to analyze the lake.[12]

Envision the lake of the education system is failing half its students. Now, we would ask: might the system itself be the reason why half its students fail so consistently? If so, how? Now, imagine a world with five lakes around your house, with half its students failing. Imagine five lakes around your house, and half the fish drift belly-up. Now what? We say it's time to test the groundwater.[13]

The groundwater represents the policies, practices, and systems built into American society that are designed to be permanent and inflexible, granting legal rights and advantages to a dominant group of people. In the case of the United States, this dominant group is white in physical appearance. "In America, race is the primary tool and the visible decoy, the front man, for caste. It is the powerful infrastructure that holds each group in its place."[14] This American groundwater, or system of caste, enables resources, respect, authority, potential, rank, worth, and value to be assigned to whiteness and disassociated with blackness.[15] Admittedly, this understanding of American history is not agreed upon by all. It is even viewed as dangerous by some who are uncomfortable addressing the topic of race. Yet, I implore us to acknowledge historical facts and work towards a better future.

United Believers Community Church in South Kansas City, led by the Rev. Darron Edwards,[16] partnering with the Hickman Mills School District is using the five steps above to build partnerships and impact the community. They are establishing unprecedented partnerships with law enforcement, clergy, businesses, and economic developers, among others. They are providing technology for students, supporting virtual learning pods, providing clothing and school supplies. Additionally, they are leading courageous conversations and advocating for racial equity in church, school, and community. Intentional partnerships are necessary to address complex social problems; a groundwater analysis makes that possible.[17] Importantly, Rev. Edwards is building unity and helping to drive electoral victories, policy changes, leadership development, and unprecedented collaborations across the city.

Main Points to Remember

Five Steps to Partnering with School and Community Leaders

1. Learn the history of your community.

2. Build relationships with persons of peace.

3. Identify community assets and challenges.

4. Understand underlying systemic causes of problems.

5. Co-develop immediate and longer-term systemic solutions.

As you analyze the groundwater in your community and connect with community, school, and church partners, consider the following questions to discuss with your team, neighbors, or group of concerned citizens.

Questions for Discussion and Action

What is the history of your community? How can you understand it more deeply?

Who are the persons of peace you can reach out to and begin
to build a relationship with?

What are the greatest assets and challenges your community is
facing today?

How might you begin to understand if systemic disparities ex-
ist in your school systems?

Chapter 3

Partnering for Self-Determination

Kujichagulia (koo–gee–cha–goo–LEE–yah)

To define, name, create, and speak for
one's self.

The Ibo village on the western coast of Africa in Nigeria was a bustling village of commerce that attracted people from all over "southeastern Nigeria coming to trade for the Ibo's cotton, corn and yams." The Aro tribe in southern Nigeria, who had an alliance with European slave traders, "brought European goods such as guns, cloth and hats to trade." They also captured young Africans as slaves for European traders. A boy named Equiano and his sister were enslaved for this purpose. In 1755, at the age of ten, "Equiano and his sister were both taken out of their neighborhood and traded by their captors."[1] After their kidnapping, Equiano and his sister never saw each other again.

Olaudah Equiano (o-lah-*oo*-day ek-wee-*ah*-no), author, abolitionist, husband, and former slave, was an extraordinary figure of the eighteenth century. According to his autobiography, *The Interesting Narrative of the Life of Olaudah Equiano*, he was born in 1745 "into the Ibo tribe in the Nigerian Village of Isseke,"[2] in what is now southeastern Nigeria.

> He was enslaved at the age of eleven and sold to English slave traders, who took him on the Middle Passage to the West Indies. Within a few days, he was taken to Virginia and sold to a local planter. After about a month in Virginia Michael Henry Paschal, an officer in the British Royal Navy who renamed him Gustavus Vassa and brought him to London, purchased him. In 1762, at the end of the Seven Years' War he was sold again to the West Indies, yet they survived and saved enough money to buy his own freedom in 1766.[3]

Equiano's story is extraordinary because he not only survived ten years of slavery in the West Indies, America, and Europe; he also bought his freedom and wrote about his experiences at a time when few former slaves had the education or means to write and publish autobiographies. Equiano's life as a slave, his spiritual journey, and his life after slavery as an abolitionist and author is an example of what it means to define one's self, name one's self, create for one's self, and speak for one's self in the midst of community.

Equiano's abolitionist work reached its height in 1788 when "he presented an antislavery petition to England's Queen Charlotte and an abolitionist petitioned the British Parliament to end the slave trade."[4] In 1789, he published his autobiography, *The Interesting Narrative of the Life of Olaudah Equiano.* His hope was to further the abolitionist movement and to inspire others such as John Wesley, founder of the Methodist movement who read his autobiography. The slave trade would not officially end in Britain until 1807, but Equiano felt his abolitionist cause was a secular conversion as significant as his spiritual conversion on October 6, 1774, had been. Equiano died on March 31, 1797, at the age of fifty-two. When Equiano died he was probably one of the wealthiest and certainly the most famous person of African descent in the Atlantic World.[5] Ultimately, Equiano's life is an example for all to hail of courage, perseverance, and faith amid challenge. This is self-determination.

We can also think of the value of self-determination as citizenship, as defined by Dr. Eric Lu, "not in terms of documentation, status and passport holding."[6] We mean it in the broader ethical sense of being a member of the body and a contributor to the community. In a word, belonging. And when we think about self-determination in those terms, we can adapt this very simple equation, which is that power plus belonging, equal self-determination or full citizenship. That to live like a citizen in this deepest way is both to be powerful and fulfilled. Radical belonging of each person regardless of their class, ethnicity, culture, color, gender, sexuality, or success creates community. So those two halves of the equation of self-determination are super important: power and belonging.

Likewise, Dan Yarnell in his essay titled "The Spirit Says 'Yes': Exploring the Essence of Being Church in the 21st Century" describes church as "worship, a shared life in fellowship, regular engagement with the scriptures, holistic discipleship, and communitas, a sacramental way of life, and missional."[7] In other words, the church is not just a physical or virtual place, but a way of being in relationship and covenant with a community of people. The safety and trust of community enables physical, spiritual, mental, and social self-determination of humanity. Regardless of one's faith beliefs and beyond the daily stressors of life, self-determination enables individual uniqueness and unity.

Importantly, as part of self-determination we must acknowledge that racism and capitalism have influenced all of US society since the inception of the US as a nation, and the church is no exception. According to Bishop Woodie W. White, the first African American bishop in The United Methodist Church, "American Methodism has always struggled with its commitment on the one hand to combat and challenge racism and prejudice, and its accommodation to racism on the other."[8] Values such as authenticity, mutuality, experience, and self-expression are essential to building a foundation of trust as diverse groups journey together. Importantly, becoming color-blind is not the goal. God created each person uniquely, so differences should be celebrated and embraced as beautiful and agents of growth for all people. God often uses people different from us to bring about transformation in our thoughts, assumptions, and actions.

Education and Self-Determination

Third grade has been identified as important to a student's self-determination. It is the final year children are learning to read, after which students are "reading to learn." If they are not proficient readers when they begin fourth grade, as much as half of the curriculum they will be taught will be incomprehensible to them.[9]

In 2015, roughly two out of three fourth graders failed to score proficient in reading. The percentages of non-proficient readers are even higher when looking at specific racial/ethnic groups: 82 percent of African American fourth-graders were reading below proficiency, along with 79 and 78 percent of Latino and Native American students, respectively.

Gaps in reading proficiency are also large between students who receive free or reduced-price lunch (a measure of family income), at 79 percent non-proficient compared to students who did not receive free or reduced-price lunch, at 48 percent non-proficient.[10]

A long-term study by the Annie E. Casey Foundation found that students who were not proficient in reading by the end of third grade were four times more likely to drop out of high school than proficient readers. In fact, 88 percent of students who failed to earn a high school diploma were struggling readers in third grade.[11]

The nation's high school graduation rate is up to approximately 88 percent, with the average state graduation rates in the 2017–2018 academic year ranging from 74 percent to 94 percent, according to data reported by 17,404 ranked schools in the 2020 *U.S. News and World Report*'s Best High Schools rankings.[12] A high school graduation rate is an indicator of how well a school is serving all of its students, with the rate calculated by analyzing the proportion of students who started high school in ninth grade that graduate four years later. Unfortunately, this data indicated that 12 percent of students fail to graduate even in the US, the wealthiest nation in the world.

We can do better. We must do better, beginning at birth through third grade, to and through high school, to enable self-determination.

As I write this, my fellow parents and I have spent the last few days in angst at the prospect of reverting to all-virtual instruction as COVID-19 cases and hospitalizations are on the rise again after the past eight months of mask-wearing, sanitizing, and physical distancing. None of us relish the prospect of online learning again, but we care about the safety of students and staff. Many of us have family members who are high risk due to underlying health issues and are absolutely frightened to gather in groups under these conditions. While these are squarely health challenges, they are also community challenges, which makes them faith challenges.

Communities across the United States are facing challenges of remote learning as K-12 schools have shifted to online classes or been forced to go remote after students or staff tested positive for COVID-19 early in the term. Many of these schools faced similar problems in the spring. An analysis of Pew Research Center data collected in early April 2020 finds that 59 percent of parents with lower incomes who had children in schools that were remote at the time said their children would likely face digital obstacles such as having to do their homework on a cellphone, using public wifi to finish homework, or not having a computer at home.[13]

Overall, 38 percent of parents with children whose K-12 schools closed in the spring of 2020 said that their child was very or somewhat likely to face technology challenges. In addition, parents with middle incomes were about twice as likely as parents with higher incomes to report anticipating issues.

So how can we respond to build self-determination?

- Care for neighbors as ourselves.

- Set universal goals.

- Utilize targeted approaches to meet the unique needs of students.

- Embrace faith values to fuel support for each student.

Building self-determination starts as simply as caring for neighbors as one's self despite differences of race, class, and background. A collective understanding of mission in a community is the same energy needed for success in education. This is a vision of targeted universalism, as popularized by john a. powell.[14]

Targeted universalism in K-12 education defines universal goals such as 100 percent of third graders reading on their grade level. This goal is the same for every student. Yet, how each student gets to the goal will vary.

Targeted universalism rejects a "one size fits all" strategy, which is likely to ignore the reality that different groups are situated differently relative to the institutions and resources of society, and that each individual child is unique. It is an approach to learning and education, whether secular or spiritual, that embraces difference and rejects the temptation of treating everyone the same, with the same curriculum, resources, and the same support. "With an unwavering commitment to the universal goal, targeted universalism platforms require a diversity of strategies to advance all people toward it. It is not narrowly concerned with the disparities between groups."[15] To be effective, a commitment to targeted universalism, or in faith language, a covenant, should be adopted. A covenant is an agreement; a commitment for all students to thrive.

The United Methodist Church Social Principles also provide direction. While these are not church law they represent the prayerful and earnest efforts of the General Conference to speak to issues in the contemporary world from a sound biblical and theological foundation that is in keeping with the best of our United Methodist traditions. The Social Principles are thus a call to faithfulness and to social engagement and intended to be instructive and persuasive in the best of the prophetic spirit. Moreover, they challenge all members of The United Methodist Church to engage in deliberative reflection and encourage intentional dialogue between faith and practice.

We declare that all individuals, no matter their circumstances or social standing, are entitled to basic human rights and freedoms. These rights are grounded in God's gracious act in creation (Gen 1:27), and they are revealed fully in Jesus's incarnation of divine love. As a church, we will work to protect these rights and freedoms within the church and to reform the structures of society to ensure that every human being can thrive. . . . Governments must be held responsible for guaranteeing human rights and liberties; such responsibilities include ensuring that all people have access to affordable, high-quality education, regardless of age, gender, ethnicity, economic status or any other divisive marker.[16]

Main Points to Remember

- Self-determination is the ability to define, name, create, and speak for one's self.

- Power plus belonging, equal self-determination or full citizenship. Radical belonging of each person regardless of their class, ethnicity, culture, color, gender, sexuality, or success creates community.

- Church as worship, a shared life in fellowship, regular engagement with the scriptures, holistic discipleship, and communitas is a sacramental way of life, and missional vehicle of self-determination.

- Third grade has been identified as important to a student's self-determination. It is the final year children are learning to read, after which students are "reading to learn."

- Self-determination starts as simply as caring for neighbors as one's self despite differences of race, class, and background.

- To be effective, a commitment to targeted universalism, or in faith language, a covenant, should be adopted. A covenant is an agreement; a commitment for all students to thrive.

Questions for Discussion and Action

As we continue a journey toward self-determination, consider the following questions to discuss with your team, neighbors, or group of concerned citizens.

How does self-determination impact students and families in your community?

Which students have the strongest self-determination? Who has the least?

How are students and families given an opportunity to define themselves and their needs?

How are students and families given an opportunity to create space, programs, and policies to meet their needs?

How are students and families given an opportunity to speak for themselves and advocate for their hopes and desires?

How will you commit and covenant to ensure all students thrive?

Chapter 4

Partnering by Collective Work and Responsibility

Ujima (oo–GEE–mah)

> To build and maintain our community together and make our brother's and sister's problems our problems and to solve them together.

Leaders in education, faith organizations, and local communities are being challenged like never before through the COVID-19 pandemic, racial strife, and politics wracking the US. Yet, despite these challenges, talented teachers, leaders, and coaches have a gift for noticing and cultivating natural talent in others. They are driven to maximize the potential of every student and athlete they serve. They love to help them believe in and get excited about their potential. Often, they see talents and strengths in people before others notice. They have the insight to see what people do best and which subjects, sports, or positions they will be good at. Excellence, not average, is their gauge and quest for every student or athlete. Importantly, the goal is not every student or athlete getting an A or winning championships. Their goal is maximizing each individual's potential. This leads to mastering skills, developing strengths, and managing weaknesses.

My daughter Alexis is blessed to have teachers and coaches who see her potential and build on her strengths. At the age of three, Alexis started learning gymnastics and competed at her first gymnastics meet at the age of six. Alexis has always loved to turn cartwheels, jump on trampolines, and run around the gym. While gymnastics started as just a fun activity for Alexis, five years later, it's become a way to cultivate skills, build confidence, and grow potential.

Coaches Chad, Alexis, and Kate introduced Alexis to gymnastics and provided opportunities for her to grow during each practice and meet. In particular, Coach Alexis helped Alexis to gain confidence in her abilities and pushed her to master fundamental skills. She sees her talent. At a time when Alexis was experiencing self-doubt, Coach Alexis stepped in and inspired Alexis to master skills consistently, not just go through the motions. She takes a personal interest in Alexis and fosters enthusiasm for gymnastics. Importantly, coach Alexis is African American, a former gymnast, and a gifted coach. Our daughter, Alexis, is African American and a gymnast. She sees herself in Coach Alexis. Their special relationship reminds me that having role models who are caring adults can foster engagement and hope in students. This is Ujima, collective work and responsibility.

Coaches and school leaders know there are many elements that impact student achievement in school and in life. Specifically, we know that outcome measures like winning medals or standardized test scores don't sufficiently measure talent, aptitude, or potential. We must keep seeking other relevant and timely data that can support students' and schools' efforts to prepare students to succeed in school and life. How do we do this?

Four Steps to Partnering with Students through Strengths

1. Begin with a growth mindset.

2. Praise the process.

3. Strive for excellence.

4. Gather feedback.

First, We Must Begin with a Growth Mindset

One clue to this mindset comes from Dr. Carol Dweck, author of *Mindset: The New Psychology of Success*[1] and her TED Talk "The Power of Believing That You Can Improve."[2] Dr. Dweck found in her research that people are born with unique genetic makeups, meaning we are all naturally better at some things than others. However, a growth mindset trusts that individuals can always learn, grow, develop, and even exceed other people's natural talents. This is where coaches and teachers play a crucial role in shaping an athlete or student's confidence and belief in what's possible. By having high expectations and providing feedback, people begin to believe in themselves. Importantly, these expectations are not about the outcomes, but rather the activities like practice time, study time, and commitment to getting better. These are the actions that people can control. Therefore, it is crucial that "teachers who understand the growth mindset do everything in their power to unlock that learning,"[3] and provide an atmosphere that fosters opportunity to practice, receive feedback, and practice again.

Second, We Must Praise the Process

In her TED Talk, Dr. Dweck shares the story of "a high school in Chicago where students had to pass a certain number of courses to graduate, and if they didn't pass a course, they got the grade 'Not Yet.' And I thought that was fantastic, because if you get a failing grade, you think, I'm nothing, I'm nowhere. But if you get the grade 'Not Yet,' you understand that you're on a learning curve. It gives you a path into the future."[4]

As students and athletes learn, the role of coaches, teachers, and caring adults is not just applauding outcomes like winning or losing but rather "praising the process [of learning] that kids engage in, their effort, their strategies, their focus, their perseverance, their improvement. This process of praise creates kids who are hardy and resilient."[5] This is what builds enthusiasm for school or sports or other activities. Engaged students feel they are contributing to their own growth and that of their class or team. As a result, they are hopeful about the future and goal oriented. They can overcome obstacles, bounce back from losses, study harder next time, and know they can make progress toward their goals.

Third, Help Students Strive for Excellence in All They Do

Excellence is found in refining skills, learning new information, and working toward mastery in people's areas of strengths. One of the ways the best coaches and teachers keep students motivated is by finding ways to measure their performance on short-term goals that can lead to longer-term goals. In the case of academics, in our daughter's second-grade class her teacher measures individual advancement on reading levels. When students master a level and are ready to move up there is celebration. Mastering a reading level can take a few weeks or several months. For our son Aaron, who loves basketball, he measures work-habit goals with consecutive days of skill practice. For our son Isaac, it's subject-area mastery of music scores on his trumpet. These metrics help them to see their skill developing in real time.

Fourth, Gather Student Feedback

Since 2009 Gallup has helped thousands of schools intentionally gather student feedback as part of their model for student success. "Students from schools that opted to participate in the survey have completed nearly 5 million surveys since the Gallup Student Poll pilot was launched in 2009."[6]

The Gallup Student Poll provides actionable data that help leaders foster a growth mindset, praise students' process for learning, and measure holistic success. Importantly, students' engagement and hope for the future are linked to achievement, grades, absenteeism, and plans after high school.[7] Helping students clarify and set goals toward what they'd like to do after high school is essential. After all, just like a GPS, it's impossible to get to a desired destination if you haven't clearly defined where you want to arrive. Goals help students focus on the journey toward achievements, meaning they allocate their time better and remain motivated during times when they may feel discouraged.

The Gallup Student Poll includes four elements: engagement with school, hope for the future, entrepreneurial aspiration, and career and financial literacy. The *2016 Gallup Student Poll Snapshot Report* reveals eight important learnings about the students it surveyed:

1. Students who are involved in their school, beyond just academics, including clubs, sports, and other activities are more hopeful, engaged and have better academic success.

2. Student interest and commitment is typically highest with younger children and declines as students get older and develop other interests outside of school. So, to keep students engaged takes intentional commitment.

3. While most students have a "best friend at school," most do not get to use their talents and do what they are best at every day.

4. Students who do get to use their talents every day at school are more engaged, hopeful, and feel more successful.

5. As students get older many lack a caring adult at school.

6. Students who have a plan for after high school, such as college or career, are more likely to be hopeful engaged in their education.

7. Students envision many careers as young children, including becoming an entrepreneur, but their ambition fades in high school.

8. Students who are involved in extracurricular activities, such as sports, clubs, and music, boost positive social, emotional, and academic outcomes for students.

Traditional academic measures illuminate areas of skill and areas of weakness. It also ranks students against one another. Often these rankings do little to foster a more holistic student success model and positive learning environments. In Isabel Wilkerson's book, *Caste: The Origins of Our Discontents*, she names hierarchy as a tool of a caste system. Ultimately, those at the top of the grading system receive more resources, respect, value, and assumption of potential.[8] Whether consciously or unconsciously, rankings often shape coach, teacher, and school behavior. In contrast to a high-stake testing with ranking, environments that give students feedback on their progress, the chance to practice what they do best, and develop a personal pathway to their goals in college, career, and beyond are most successful.

Importantly, goal setting with students and young adults takes a village including parents, teachers, coaches, and community support. Ewing Marion Kauffman Foundation is part of the Kansas City community committed to collaborating to rethink high school education. "By providing funding, building connections with experts and advisors, supporting local organizations that create Real World Learning opportunities, and tracking data on student outcomes after high school, the Kauffman Foundation will strengthen the KC community to support students as they navigate from high school to career."[9] This is essential because according to data provided by the National Center for Education Statistics, of every one hundred high school students in the US, only 14 earn both a 4-year college degree and career of their choice, while eighty-six students are left behind, often with student debt, without the degree or career that they desire.[10] We must do better supporting students.

When students get the opportunity to define their own goals for college and/or career they are naturally motivated to work harder and achieve milestones through internships and entrepreneurial projects. Importantly, when mentors and networks of caring adults are partners, they help with students' overall development.[11]

Talented teachers[12] and coaches who have cultivated their own skills through consistent practice and feedback can support students in their journey to discover what they do best and develop and apply their strengths every day. The sooner students begin to learn more about themselves and what they do best, the more prepared they will be to succeed in school, sports, and life. As a certified Gallup Strengths coach, I recognize that coaches and teachers, who intentionally spot and develop talent in their students and athletes, know that relationships are essential for learning. As coaches and teachers model care and deep empathy, students respond with increased effort, motivation, and joy. And parents, like me, are very grateful.

What's Holding Students Back?

Every person is born with talents, gifts, skills. A talent, as defined by decades of research by the Gallup research, is "a natural way of thinking, feeling or behaving. A strength is the result of taking that talent and, with investment—skills, knowledge and practice—using it to consistently provide near-perfect performance in a given activity"[13]—create strengths.

Developing Talents into Strengths

- Name talents

- Practice talents

- Demonstrate talents as strengths

First, people, especially children, are not always aware of their talents. Talents are so innate, natural, and deep-seated. They are not acquired skills. Talents are so inherent and ever-present that you might not even realize you have them. In fact, people typically think that whatever talents they have, everybody has. A student talented in math thinks that everyone can easily do math problems. An athlete talented in sports assumes kicking and catching a ball are easy to do. Yet, if it's not your natural talent, these natural ways of thinking, feeling, or behaving are not instinctive.

Second, merely telling a child he has talent and can succeed is not enough. To believe he can succeed, he has to actually experience success. This success often comes when he is using his innate talents. Confidence in ability influences success, and success influences confidence or self-belief of ability. Understanding this interaction is essential. That's why efforts to increase self-esteem don't work if they're not demonstrated in practice. It's through consistent effort focused in areas of talent that children learn from themselves that they are talented and can succeed.[14]

Third, students need opportunities to demonstrate their talents and develop them into strengths—consistently demonstrating near-perfect performance in a given activity. One of these opportunities for students talented academically is through Advanced Placement (AP) and International Baccalaureate (IB) courses. AP and IB courses are a powerful means of disrupting achievement gaps among the most talented students, but too many "low-income students and students of color are missing out."[15] It turns out that according to The Education Trust "more than half a million low-income students and students of color are 'missing' from AP and IB participation—students who would benefit from these advanced opportunities if they participated at the same rate as other students."[16]

Why Is Investing in Talented Students So Important?

The economic costs of not recognizing talent and encouraging education both to individuals and to society are significant. In evidence from the McKinsey & Company report, titled "The Economic Impact of the Achievement Gap in America's Schools," economists clearly demonstrate that the lack of a college education will increasingly lock American citizens out of the middle class. These achievement gaps in America produce a substantial drag on our economy, contributing to what one report called a "permanent national recession."[17] And there are also societal impacts such as a decrease in physical and emotional well-being, less economic stability, and overall fewer options in life for individuals with less education. We know that the strongest predictor of whether a student will achieve success in college is whether she had a rich and rigorous course of study in high school.[18] Here's how schools are investing in talented students,[19] as detailed in The Education Trust:

1. Begin with Data. Schools are gathering and honestly interrogating which students are not gaining access to advanced coursework. This has identified an opportunity gap for students of color and from lower socioeconomic households.

2. Expand entry requirements. Policies and practices for advanced course enrollment are expanding to include diverse qualitative and quantitative data.

3. Expand student awareness. Data shows that racial and ethnic minorities and students from lower socioeconomic groups lack information about the benefits of advanced course work and how to access the courses successfully.

4. Believe all students can be successful in advanced courses and ensure inclusion of underrepresented students all along the way. "Many times unsaid expectations about who is 'AP material' get conveyed to students. For example, underrepresented students often don't feel welcome in AP/IB classrooms because no other students who share their background or skin color are taking AP/IB classes."[20]

5. Set annual enrollment goals to ensure all student groups are represented in advanced courses. Then, make the operational changes necessary to achieve success. "Determining whatever changes in staff assignments, master schedules, professional development, and staff supports are necessary to build a culture of high achievement for all students."[21]

These data indicate there is a clear opportunity gap for talented students to access high-quality rigorous high school courses. We must close the opportunity gap in education if we want to close achievement gaps.

This is the work of every school, leader, teacher, parent, and community member. Collectively, we "must commit to eliminating the opportunity gap if we are going to build a stronger, safer and more prosperous nation."[22] One of the ways to close these gaps is AP/IB programs. Data suggest that "African Americans and Latinos in AP/IB/honors classes . . . (1) benefitted socially, emotionally and academically from the program, (2) the participants felt affirmed and safe in groups of racial affinity, (3) being clustered with other African Americans and Latinos in AP/IB/honors classes eliminated the participants' feelings of isolation and hypervisibility, and (4) the participants valued the relationship and support provided by the High Achievement Program Coordinator."[23] This is an example of collective work and responsibility that will last for generations.

Main Points to Remember

- Teachers, coaches, and school leaders know there are many elements that impact student achievement in school and in life. Specifically, we know that outcome measures like winning medals or standardized test scores don't sufficiently measure talent, aptitude, or potential. We must keep seeking other relevant and timely data that can support students' and schools' efforts to prepare students to succeed in school and life.

- Four steps to partnering with students through strengths.
  - Begin with a Growth Mindset.
  - Praise the Process.
  - Strive for Excellence.
  - Gather Feedback.

- To investing in talented students:
  - Begin with data.
  - Expand entry requirements.
  - Expand student awareness.
  - Believe all students can be successful in advanced courses.
  - Set annual enrollment goals.

Questions for Discussion and Action

Consider the following questions to discuss with your team, neighbors, or group of concerned citizens.

How can you use your collective strengths as an organization to support students in developing their talents and strengths?

How can you support student interests in clubs, sports, and other activities?

How can the school day be restructured to enable students to use their talents and do what they are best at every day?

How can caring adults better support students inside and outside of school?

What steps can you take to help students define and prepare for college or a career?

How can you nurture entrepreneurship?

How can you advocate for student success, including AP and IB courses, to disrupt high-end achievement gaps for students who may be missing out?

Chapter 5

Partnering through Cooperative Economics

Ujamaa (oo–JAH–mah)

To build and maintain stores, shops,
and other businesses and to profit
from them together.

Go to the people. Live among them,
Learn from them,
Love them.
Start with what they know,
Build on what they have:
But of the best leaders, When their task is done,
The people will remark, "We have done it ourselves."

—Ancient Chinese Proverb[1]

It was a brisk Chicago spring day in March 2020, days before the COVID-19 pandemic was declared in the US. We spent the afternoon visiting North Lawndale, a working-class African American neighborhood west of downtown.

North Lawndale was organized in 1857 as part of Cicero Township. In 1869 the eastern portion was annexed to Chicago, and in 1889 the west portion became part of the city. July 21, 1899, Ernest Hemingway, winner of both the Pulitzer and Nobel prizes, was born within the Town of Cicero.[2] Several industries developed in the rapidly growing community, the most notable being the Sears, Roebuck and Co. mail-order facility and administrative headquarters, which opened in 1905. "North Lawndale doubled its population between 1910 and 1920, from 46,226 to 93,750, and added 18,000 more people by 1930, when almost half of the 112,000 residents were Russian Jews. Roosevelt Road became the best-known Jewish commercial street in Chicago."[3]

By the mid 1950s North Lawndale's population began to shift as people migrated west of downtown Chicago. White and Jewish families moved out, while African Americans moved in. "The 1950s were a decade of 'white flight,' as the white population dropped from 87,000 in 1950 to less than 11,000 in 1960 and the African-American population grew from 13,000 to more than 113,000. By the 1960s North Lawndale was at its all-time population high, nearly 125,000, and was 91% African-American." The population grew, while physical and social infrastructure lagged.

> In 1966, the neighborhood's poverty prompted Martin Luther King, Jr. to pick North Lawndale as the base for the northern civil rights movement. Residents found King's visit highly symbolic: his stay attracted much attention, but little tangible change. Riots followed the assassination of Martin Luther King, Jr. in 1968, destroying many of the stores along Roosevelt Road and accelerating a decline that led to a loss of 75% of the businesses in the community by 1970.[4]

Wayne "Coach" Gordon moved into the neighborhood in the 1970s and served as a basketball coach at the local high school and started what became the Lawndale Church.[5] Our visit kicked off our tour of Lawndale Christian Development Corporation, "a developer, partner and catalyst for community revitalization in the North Lawn-dale community."[6]

By "loving in a holistic way" and seeking to meet local needs, the church became a real estate developer. Over the last few decades, LCDC has supported the development of a youth center, learning center, pizza parlor, urgent care clinic, health center, eye clinic, recovery center, senior daycare center, social services, cafe, and fitness center. LCDC is active in producing affordable housing by building and renovating local properties and encouraging homeownership. LCDC continues to create new commercial development opportunities and new jobs for residents. LCDC participates in the planning efforts of the North Lawndale Community Coordinating Council to create a comprehensive community plan for the North Lawndale community.

Over thirty years, Gordon has collaborated with John Perkins and Vera Mae Perkins and their Foundation for Justice, Reconciliation & Community Development (JVMPF), a nonprofit organization that teaches and promotes the principles of Christian community development and racial reconciliation. Perkins, a Baptist minister from Mississippi, and Gordon, an evangelical minister rooted in Chicago, formed the Christian Community Development Association (CCDA) to spark transformation in communities across the country.[7]

In 2013, Gordon and Perkins wrote *Making Neighborhoods Whole: A Handbook for Christian Community Development*.[8] It lays out the eight guiding principles of CCDA, including reconciliation, redistribution, listening to the community, leadership development, and a holistic approach to building communities through relationships, economics, and empowerment.

In 2017, Perkins and Gordon wrote *Do All Lives Matter?: The Issues We Can No Longer Ignore and the Solutions We All Long For*.[9] Perkins and Gordon write, "The belief that all lives matter is at the heart of our founding documents—but we must admit that this conviction has never truly reflected reality in America. Movements such as Black Lives Matter have arisen in response to recent displays of violence and mistreatment, and some of us defensively answer back, 'All lives matter.' But do they? Really?"[10]

The investment in Ujamaa, cooperative economics, in Lawndale wasn't a sudden change. Gradually, Lawndale has changed in substantive ways—ways that change people's lives and improve the community. Here are just a few examples.

- A new youth center provides a safe place to play and learn.

- A pizza parlor provides jobs to local residents and an opportunity to further life skills.

- An urgent care, health center, and eye clinic provide affordable healthcare for all community residents regardless of income.

- A recovery center supports persons regaining health and wholeness.

- A senior daycare center provides wholistic care to seniors so family members have support.

- A cafe and fitness center provide sustainable businesses that operate in a way that protects and enhances the lives of people and the community.

These progressive changes were grounded in a commitment to the eight guiding principles of CCDA including reconciliation, redistribution, listening to the community, leadership development, and a holistic approach. It was produced by building people power and leveraging political assets. It was produced and continues to be undergirded by faith.

Cooperative economics is systemic, and it is also deeply personal. The story of Elliott Clark reminds us of the personal and societal impact of economic systems. I met Elliot Clark on one of my first days in training as a community organizer with Communities Creating Opportunity[11] in Kansas City. Here's Elliot's story as told dozens of times in public forums as he advocates for payday loan regulation.

> Elliott Clark served two tours in Vietnam, worked as a cook at a Kansas City restaurant, and owned a home with his wife, Aquila. Three days before Aquila was eligible for full benefits at her new job, she slipped and broke her ankle. Though Elliott had been a faithful, good-standing client of his bank for years, he was not approved for the loan he needed to pay the hospital bill. With no other option, he turned to a payday loan to foot the bill.
>
> The massive interest rate of the loan dug Elliott into an even deeper financial hole. That one payday loan multiplied into five. He accumulated $50,000 in interest from only $2,500 worth of loans. Elliott and his wife lost their car and their home. He eventually received a lump-sum disability check from the VA, and managed to pay off the debt collectors.
>
> Communities Creating Opportunity (CCO) connected with Elliot and disseminated his story. He was featured in *TIME*, on ABC News, and in local media such as *The Kansas City Star*, significantly raising awareness of the predatory lending crisis in poor minority areas of American municipalities. CCO, committed to empowering residents personally affected by injustices, also developed Elliott as a leader. He became cochair of CCO's "Stop the Debt Trap" campaign in 2016.

Elliott is now a staunch advocate against the exorbitant interest rates predatory lenders offer folks with no better option for a small-dollar, short-term loan. "I want to tell people now that hey, your voice has to be heard because if you don't say something then you are always suffering in silence; and there's too many people here to help you," Elliott said.[12] Ujamaa is to build and maintain community and to benefit from them together.

Main Points to Remember

- Ujamaa, cooperative economics, is to build and maintain community including stores, shops, and other businesses and to profit from them together.

- Ujamaa requires us to "Go to the people. Live among them, Learn from them, Love them. Start with what they know, Build on what they have: But of the best leaders, When their task is done, The people will remark, 'We have done it ourselves.'"[13]

- The investment in Ujamaa in Lawndale wasn't a sudden change. Gradually, Lawndale has changed in substantive ways—ways that change people's lives and improve the community.

- Ujamaa is systemic, and it is also deeply personal. This story of Elliott Clark reminds us of the personal and societal impact of economic systems.

Questions for Discussion and Action

As we continue a journey toward cooperative economics, consider the following questions to discuss with your team, neighbors, or group of concerned citizens:

Who are the local block captains or "persons of peace" in your neighborhood who are essential for partnership and collaboration?

How does your organization intentionally seek a just distribution of resources and work for justice in underserved portions of your community?

How does your organization intentionally help to build and maintain Black-owned stores, shops, and other businesses and to circulate wealth within the community instead of witnessing capital only flowing outside the community?

How can your organization advocate against the exorbitant interest rates of predatory lenders in your community?

How does your organization intentionally ensure that people are able to help themselves after they have been helped? Oftentimes, organizations, particularly in asset-deprived communities, create dependency on charity instead of economic independence.

Chapter 6

Partnering for Purpose

Nia (nee–YAH)

> A commitment to the collective voca-
> tion of building, developing and de-
> fending our community, its culture and
> history in order to add to . . . the good
> and beauty in the world.[2]

The reason for which something exists or is done, made, used.[1]

Della Lamb began in 1897 to provide childcare to working Ital-
ian immigrant families in Kansas City. The Methodists founded Della
Lamb more than 120 years ago with the intent to assist the marginalized. As Della Lamb interacted with families, other fundamental needs
were identified including housing, food, clothing, and jobs, among
others. Today, Della Lamb continues to be a valued community partner that "serves the needs of 1,500-plus low-income families every day
in northeast Kansas City, Missouri, and the urban core. . . . Emergency
Services include rent and utility assistance; use of a food pantry, senior-
related services including home-bound meal deliveries, transportation

for medical services, groceries, or to work; school supplies; and groceries and gifts to make the holidays special."[3]

I first encountered Della Lamb while working with the Kuomba Pamoja ministry of Central United Methodist Church in Kansas City. It developed into a new church start of African immigrants, with over two hundred members at its one-year anniversary. It began as a choir and grew to offer an English-Swahili worship service on Sunday mornings, a translated Swahili-into-English worship service on Saturdays, and eventually relocated to become its own congregation in a United Methodist Church building. The evangelist and pastor, Rev. Riziki Lubula, came to the United States in 2013 with her husband and seven children after living for thirteen years in refugee camps in countries bordering the Democratic Republic of the Congo. The Lubula family settled in northeastern Kansas City and became connected with Central United Methodist Church with the support of Della Lamb.

Della Lamb is just one example of an organization exemplifying the Kwanzaa principle of purpose through "collective vocation," or "shared responsibility to build, develop and defend our community, its culture and history for the purpose of . . . preserv[ing] it and pass[ing] it on to future generations."[4] In addition to emergency services Della Lamb fulfills its purpose through early childhood education, and providing children food and educational experiences.[5] It offers youth, ages five to seventeen, experiences in camping, sports, tutoring, and homework assistance.[6] In Kwanza, purpose includes providing education of many types for people of all ages, not just a conventional school setting. That is part of the point of this chapter—that education extends beyond the school walls. Education happens through life experiences with caring people.

Importantly, in recent years one of the growing programs of Della Lamb is Refugee Immigrant Resettlement, "More than 600 persons have been resettled in Kansas City since 2014, most from eastern or tribal African countries. Refugees are provided housing, furnishings, assistance with employment opportunities, employment training, legal/governmental support, . . . and life skill studies."[7] Ryan Hudnall, executive director of Della Lamb, said in a recent article by the Missouri Methodist, "My prayer is for Kansas City to become known as the city of hospitality—the city that cares for its neighbors." This requires partnerships with employers and landlords, churches and donors to help those in need. "We say to our clients, 'You are refugees no more. Welcome home,'" Hudnall said.[8]

In the summer of 2020, over six hundred clergy and people of faith walked across New England in solidarity with the Faith in Action coalition in New Hampshire to mourn the deaths of people killed in immigration custody and to grieve the violent and unjust ways the US government treated immigrants, refugees, and asylum seekers. Subsequently, clergy delivered a letter to all presidential primary candidates signed by over one thousand clergy and leaders of faith institutions from across the Faith in Action network. The letter read,

> As faith leaders of diverse traditions from across the United States, we have been organizing, responding, and offering pastoral care to the members of our congregations and communities that have been under direct attack by repressive immigration policies and harmful rhetoric. Our shared faith values of recognizing the dignity of all, family, community and compassion inspire this work and compel us to reach out to you. . . .
>
> We are writing to urge you to speak out clearly and boldly in your presidential campaign on behalf of immigrants, refugees and asylum-seekers in this time of increasing fear-mongering and growing nationalism in our country. We urge you to take a moral stance as presidential candidate [sic] to unravel the immigration enforcement system and protect all immigrant families. . . .
>
> We believe moral leadership on immigration requires the points outlined above as a centerpiece of your campaign, and call on all candidates to deliver a major speech on your immigration platform. We believe that, by leading from a place of love and compassion, you can help begin to heal the wounds of racism and xenophobia which have diminished us all.[9]

In today's world filled with the challenges of pandemic and protest, health disparities and political insurrection, individuals, congregations, and organizations must speak up and advocate for what is right, what is just, and what will benefit the people most in need.

> Lift every voice and sing
> Till earth and heaven ring,
> Ring with the harmonies of Liberty.
>
> —J. Rosamond Johnson and James Weldon Johnson[10]

These words begin a deeply inspiring congregational hymn that we sang every first Sunday at St. James United Methodist Church. Many African Americans will readily recognize these words and hold them in their hearts. They are from the poem and hymn "Lift Every Voice and Sing," which for generations has been known as the anthem of hope and unity during trying times. Now is the moment for these words to ring out and be lifted up by everyone. This is our purpose, lifting every voice. Believing in our own value and that of organizations enables a connection to a mission and purpose that's bigger than us. Our collective vocation, the liberation of people and community, is our mutual calling. This demonstrates the Kwanza principle of purpose "A commitment to the collective vocation of building, developing and defending our community, its culture and history in order to add to . . . the good and beauty in the world."[11]

In 1920, the 19th Amendment granted US women full voting rights.[12] In 1956, the General Conference of The Methodist Church approved full clergy rights for women.[13] In 1964, the US Civil Rights Act outlawed racial segregation in public schools. These are examples of Nia, or partnering for purpose. Women have always been invested in America and been smart enough to vote, yet were denied the right. Women have always been filled with the Holy Spirit and called by God to lead in word, sacrament, and order, yet denied the right to ordination and full privileges as clergy within religious structures. Black and brown students have always valued academic achievement yet were hindered by inequitable policies and resources. During each of these movements, women have been prophetic witnesses to challenge oppression based upon gender and race. Women in the suffrage, clergy rights, and civil rights movements used marches, sit-ins, and public speaking instruments for their communal choir. Likewise, women today use community organizing, public pulpits, musical lyrics, and social media as tools to fight inequity.

However, the essence of these partnerships for purpose is not new. One of my favorite characters in the Bible is that of the Hebrew midwives. The midwives in biblical history were essential workers. Midwives stood in the gap between mother and child, amid life and death. In Exodus 1:15-22, midwives sabotaged the command of the Egyptian king to kill the Hebrew boys, thus preventing genocide of a nation. Ultimately, the action of the midwives foreshadowed the Israelites' liberation from slavery in Egypt and their survival as a nation. As womanist sociologist Cheryl Townsend Gilkes said, "If it wasn't for the women there would be no exodus, no Moses, no liberation of the children of Israel of which to speak."[14] Likewise, without women acting powerfully, the fulfillment of purpose within communities is at risk.

One of my favorite historical women leaders is Ella Baker, who played a critical role in the three most prominent civil rights organizations of her day: the NAACP, the Southern Christian Leadership Conference (SCLC), and the Student Non-Violent Coordinating Committee (SNCC). Through the nurturing of women in her family and the church, Baker was a courageous female leader who worked alongside the prominent male leaders of the civil rights movement and "criticized unchecked egos, objected to undemocratic structures, protested unilateral decision making, condemned elitism, and refused to nod in loyal deference to everything 'the leader' had to say. These stances often put her on the outside of the inner circle."[15] Baker believed that, "Strong people don't need strong leaders." She argued that "oppressed people did not need a messiah to deliver them from oppression; all they needed was themselves." Her message of shared leadership was in stark contrast to the SCLC's and the Black church's patriarchal model of God.[16] In Kwanza, purpose includes providing access and opportunity

to people of all genders and races, and magnifying the good and beauty
of the church, school, and community.

Main Points to Remember

- Purpose in Kwanza is "The reason for which something
  exists or is done, made, used."[17] "A commitment to the
  collective vocation of building, developing and defending
  our community, its culture and history in order to add to
  . . . the good and beauty in the world."[18]

- Della Lamb is an example of an organization exemplifying
  the Kwanzaa principle through community, culture, and
  caring.

- In Kwanza, purpose includes providing education of
  many types for people of all ages, not just a conventional
  school setting. That is part of the point of this chapter—
  that education extends beyond the school walls. Education happens through life experiences with caring people.

- Ella Baker believed, "Strong people don't need strong
  leaders." She argued that "oppressed people did not need a
  messiah to deliver them from oppression; all they needed
  was themselves." Shared leadership is essential for people
  and communitites to achieve their collective purpose.

Questions for Discussion and Action

Women have often risked their lives for liberation, inspired by divine authority, toward a collective purpose of freedom and justice. As you continue a journey toward purpose (*nia*), consider discussing the following questions with your team, neighbors, or group of concerned citizens.

Each person, generation, and organization or community is called to discover its essential purpose and then work toward it. How does your organization understand liberation as an essential purpose for your work? Who are you working to liberate? Why is this important for your legacy?

Personal purpose and social purpose can benefit one another. In light of the personal and social purpose of your organization, what's the one thing you uniquely contribute to your community?

How can you advocate for your purpose publicly following the footsteps of clergy advocating for immigrant rights?

How is your organization/community bringing good into the world through supporting job training, development, and preservation? Research clearly indicates that being able to stay employed is good for physical, mental, and spiritual health, and that unemployment—especially long-term unemployment—is associated with increases in mortality.[19]

Chapter 7

Partnering with Creativity

Kuumba (koo–OOM–bah)

> To always do as much as we can, in the
> way we can, in order to leave our com-
> munity more beautiful and beneficial
> than we inherited it.

That morning in June 1958 seemed like a typical workday; however, it would turn out to be very, very different. I was going to work—but not to the cotton fields where I had been working for several years and where she, herself, would go that day. No, I would not be bending low in the hot sun from early morning to sunset, carefully weeding the young cotton plants—a process we called chopping. Uncle Cleve, Ma Ponk's brother-in-law who owned the Ice House, had offered me the opportunity to work for the summer—that is, if my first few days worked out to his satisfaction. I never wanted to earn that admired reputation of chopping more rows than anyone else. I never wanted to learn how to sharpen my own hoe. Even though I was born into that world, I always wanted something better. I didn't know what better would look like; I just knew that I wanted something different. The problem was that "better" jobs were virtually nonexistent—that is until the job at the Ice House opened up for me.[1]

This is the true story of an unlikely entrepreneur, Uncle Cleve, a Black man who owned the only ice house in a town in the Mississippi Delta in the late 1950s, and his nephew, barely a teenager, who gained real-world experience that shaped his life. As you might expect, Uncle Cleve had many challenges as a Black business owner in the 1950s who served both Blacks and whites. This was during the Jim Crow era where laws enforced racial segregation of people in the South. Despite opposition, Cleve had an uncanny resolve, a creative vision, and an entrepreneurial spirit that enabled him to succeed.

Uncle Cleve believed more was possible as an entrepreneur, owning the ice house.[2]

An entrepreneurial spirit includes beliefs and values that guide creative behavior. It's the internal motivation that builds "grit" as defined by Angela Duckworth in her book *Grit: The Power of Passion and Perseverance*. "It's tenacity, strength, dedication, and a deep belief that one's actions can lead to progress and ultimately to success"[3] like Uncle Cleve. It is a faith in what's unseen yet believed. It's a commitment fueled by lifelong curiosity and creativity. Importantly, people are not born entrepreneurs or with a particular mindset. An entrepreneurial spirit is developed and enhanced through real-world learning opportunities at home, in classrooms, with organizations (such as churches), and in communities. An entrepreneurial spirit can lead to a set of skills such as collaboration, risk-taking, and deep listening that enable people to identify and make the most of opportunities, overcome and learn from setbacks, and succeed despite unexpected challenges.

So how do we enable creativity within communities through partnerships? A primary scriptural text for cultivating creative action is Luke 4:18-19 as inspired by Isaiah's prophecy. This text has been chosen from among the many in the Bible because Jesus's preaching focuses on doing as much as we can, in the way we can, in order to leave our community more beautiful and beneficial than we inherited it. This is Kuumba.

The Spirit of the Lord is upon me, because he has anointed me to bring good news to the poor. He has sent me to proclaim release to the captives and recovery of sight to the blind, to let the oppressed go free, to proclaim the year of the Lord's favor. (Luke 4:18-19)

Three Steps for Nurturing Creativity

1. Bring good news to the poor.

2. Proclaim release to the captives.

3. Proclaim the year of the Lord's favor.

1. Bring Good News to the Poor.

The first creative step is to bring good news to the poor. Empowerment begins from the bottom. The poor are people and communities who are often economically disadvantaged, socially impoverished, and relationally outcast. In the context of the US, a wealthy nation, the poor are also marginalized or "destitute and disadvantaged people in a wealthy environment."[4] For example, poor Black women and thus Black families are often the poorest, most destitute, and disadvantaged economically in systems of patriarchy where white men and their families are often the most powerful and wealthy. To take this a step further, a poor Black widowed woman could be socially outcast even more. Here are four practical examples to creatively bring good news (love) to the poor as adapted from pastor and practical theologian Michael L. Cook[5] and Dr. Andre Perry, author, journalist, and researcher from the Brookings Institute.[6]

Develop an **economic development ministry** that helps promote home ownership, savings, investments, and entrepreneurship.

Form **partnerships with existing organizations** like HUD Homes, Habitat for Humanity, and FHA to encourage homeownership.

Establish a **credit union within the church or community** to provide low-interest or no-interest loans to start small businesses, make short-term investments, invest in real estate, and so on.

Change the narrative and **highlight assets in your city**, beginning with people. Importantly, diverse families, neighborhoods, and students are not deficits in need of fixing. They are assets. Find ways to **celebrate the talents, strengths, and genius of people and history daily**, not just on special holidays.[7]

2. Proclaim Release to the Captives.

A second creative step is the proclamation and work of releasing captives. Release in this text is from the Greek word *aphesis*. "*Aphesis* appears in . . . Leviticus 25:10 as the translation of the Hebrew for *jubilee*, and identified . . . the 'release' as being that of debtors during a jubilee year. But Luke also uses aphesis for *forgiveness* in 24:47."[8] In other words, release can be physical, spiritual, or social liberation.

Captives are people bound physically, spiritually, or socially. In the context of the United States, one way captives can be understood is as the lower-ranked people at the bottom of a caste system. A caste system, as defined by Isabel Wilkerson in her book *Caste: The Origins of Our Discontents*, is

> an artificial construction, a fixed and embedded ranking of human value that sets the presumed supremacy of one group against the presumed inferiority of other groups on the basis of ancestry and often immutable traits, traits that would be neutral in the abstract but are ascribed life-and-death meaning in a hierarchy favoring the dominant caste whose forebears designed it. A caste system uses rigid, often arbitrary boundaries to keep the ranked groupings apart, distinct from one another and in their assigned places. . . . A caste system endures because it is often justified as divine will, originating from sacred text of the presumed laws of nature, reinforced throughout culture and passed down through the generations.[9]

In the US race is the primary tool and marker of caste. The darker a person is, the lower-ranked they are in American caste. The lighter a person is, the higher-ranked they are in the caste. Ultimately, caste is about the power differential between people and the resources, respect, and opportunity one is afforded in society. Caste, for groups of people, is typically permanent and inflexible. Caste, based on race, in America has endured for more than four hundred years. Dark-skinned people have been captive in a permanent underclass.

In addition to the racial caste, people may feel imprisoned because of their faith. Women may feel captive in systems of subordination in church and society due to their race or gender. Historically, Black women have also been bound by sexual exploitation as their bodies have been abused as the property of another since the inception of chattel slavery. Others may feel enslaved by drugs, alcohol, and the tyranny of chronic underemployment.

Proclaiming the good news in situations of physical, emotional, and social captivity must not be an add-on for our community. It is critical for the survival of individuals, communities, and students.

Students may be held captive by:

- disengaging learning environments

- a lack of physical, emotional, and psychological safety at school

- meaningless and irrelevant work and classroom discourse

- their cultural, spiritual, and/or ethnic values and practices not being acknowledged, honored, and respected

- feeling unseen, disrespected, and uncared for by adults and peers

- lack of opportunities to set and meet goals, nor recover from failure

In contrast, it is the responsibility of adults in schools and the community to:

- nurture empathy for those who experience physical, spiritual, and social challenges. Radical empathy encourages people to listen, experience, and feel the pain of others. As a result of these experiences, one's perspective and actions can be fundamentally shifted to become an advocate for equity.[10] This is the essence of love.

- teach the truthfulness of American history for remembering, reconciling, and creating an equitable future for all.

- center the voices and experiences of diverse students, families, and advocates who are closest to the margins.

- consciously remove barriers to ensure diverse students and families have access to all opportunities such as advanced coursework.

- provide restorative justice for students by eliminating the use of out-of-school suspension, which is known to increase the risk for dropout and arrest.[11] Restoration for students can include deep empathy through storytelling, listening, building relationships, and prayer. It leads to collective actions such as restorative circles, mediation, and community decision making. Effective restorative justice results in addressing the role that education systems and policies may play in promoting violence and punishment instead of restoration. Changing punitive policies can lead to greater student success.

3. Proclaim the Year of the Lord's Favor.

The third creative step is the holistic proclamation of reconciliation. In the biblical Gospel of Luke *today* is a word that is repeated. "It occurs 12 times in Luke and only 9 times in the other three gospels combined. . . . For Luke 'today' is a moment of radical change."[12] In other words, liberation is with us today, if we choose to progress together. In a world without caste, there is hope, peace, patience, kindness, opportunity, and equity for all.

Today the communities in the US that have been historically divested in are experiencing the brunt of the economic, health, and social pandemic. The COVID-19 epidemic has revealed that despite an African American president, civil rights legislation, and integration of some schools, corporations, and neighborhoods over the past sixty years, there is much work to be done. In the PBS special "The Two Nations of Black America," five characteristics emerged that define Blacks in the inner cities of America: (1) single female head of household, (2) welfare dependence, (3) marginal education (high school or less), (4) chronic unemployment, and (5) criminal recidivism (in and out of jail).[13] These ills are a result of systemic oppression, not inherently bad people, and can only be cured when Blacks and whites, young and old, poor and rich, Christians and non-Christians work together to creatively nurture the community.

In the context of the local church and community, a practical tool of creativity is community organizing. Matthew Bolton,[14] in his book *How to Resist: Turn Protest to Power*,[15] shares five principles and examples of how he has built a nationwide alliance of thousands of communities working toward justice.

Build Power: If you want to change, you need power.

Build Relationships: You build up power through relationships with other people around common interests.

Break Down Problems: You break down the big problems you face together into specific issues and identify who the decision makers are, who has the power to make the changes you need.

Take Action: Then you take action to get a reaction and build a relationship with the decision makers. If they don't agree to implement the changes then you escalate the action or turn to more creative tactics.

Celebrate Progress: Learning as you go and celebrating the small wins as you build incrementally up to the bigger issues.[16]

Main Points to Remember

- Uncle Cleve refused to let his circumstances limit his life possibilities. While the realities of living in the South influenced his opportunities, he still believed more was possible and that he could be an entrepreneur, owning the ice house.

- An entrepreneurial spirit includes "grit" as defined by Angela Duckworth in her book *Grit: The Power of Passion and Perseverance*. "It's tenacity, strength, dedication, and a deep belief that one's actions can lead to progress and ultimately to success"[17] like Uncle Cleve. It is a faith in what's unseen yet believed.

- **Three Steps for Nurturing Creativity:**
  - Bring good news to the poor.
  - Proclaim release to the captives.
  - Proclaim the year of the Lord's favor.

- **Five steps to creatively lead change in your community:**
  - ○ Build Power.
  - ○ Build Relationships.
  - ○ Break Down Problems.
  - ○ Take Action.
  - ○ Celebrate Progress.

Questions for Discussion and Action

As you seek to practice creativity in your community, school, and church, consider the following questions to discuss with your team, neighbors, or group of concerned citizens.

Who are the poor in your community? How can you creatively bring them good news?

Which students in your community may feel unseen, disrespected, and uncared for by adults and peers? How can you support them?

How can restorative justice practices be incorporated in your community?

The Freedom Quilting Bee is a quilting cooperative established in 1966 by a group of African American women in the community of Rehoboth, forty-six miles from Selma, in Wilcox County, Alabama.[19] The groups arose during the civil rights movement and shared resources, supported one another, earned income collectively, and saved enough to buy land and a factory. How can you encourage creative entrepreneurship among students and families in your community?

How can you creatively lead change in your community?

- Who can you build power with?

- Who can you build relationships with?

- What problems need to be solved first?

- What action can be taken first?

- How will you celebrate progress?

Chapter 8

Partnering in Faith

Imani (ee–MAH–nee)

> To believe with all our heart in God,
> our people, our parents, our teachers,
> our leaders, and the righteousness
> and victory of our struggle.

January 6, 2021, is a day in US history that should never be forgotten. The day began with the country anxiously awaiting the outcome of two Senate run-off elections in the state of Georgia. The balance of power was at stake between the Democratic and the Republican parties. After forty-eight hours of votes trickling in by county, the Rev. Raphael Warnock and Jon Ossoff were declared victorious. Democrats would control both the Senate and House of Representatives for the first time in ten years.[1] A day that was extraordinary was also stoked by verbal and physical violence by insurgents. A "Save America Rally" included President Donald Trump "telling supporters to 'stop the steal' of the election, urging them to head to the Capitol to demonstrate against Congress certifying President-elect Joe Biden's victory. Among the crowd's battle cries was, 'Fight for Trump! Fight for Trump! Fight for Trump!'"[2] The day ended with a fatality after the US Capitol was decimated by the angry mob.[3] In what was already a historic day, there were also 3,844 US deaths from the COVID-19 pandemic.[4] Throughout the day my emotions swung from joy to anger, optimism to frustration in a matter of minutes. What sustained me on this day and in the days to come is Imani. It is a faith in God and people to collectively address violence and heal the underlying causes of the January 6 insurrection.

Historically, faith has given people the ability to trust God (or a higher power) and one another in the midst of adversity. There is a deep knowing that trust is built through dialogue and action across time, geography, cultures, and experience. Trusting then can enable endurance and liberation to overcome violence and heal underlying causes of conflict. This is not a confidence in quick change, but in the deliberate and sustained work of empathy, collaboration, and liberation for all. As a result, no matter what happens politically, through faith one can maintain hope. As quoted by Dr. Martin Luther King Jr., "The arc of the moral universe is long but it bends toward justice."[5]

Hope, dialogue, and collective action among Jews, Muslims, and Christians are examples of Imani despite struggle. One of the reasons this faith is possible is because Judaism, Islam, and Christianity in some way all trace their beginnings to the biblical characters of Hagar and Sarah—the founding mothers of these faiths.[6] There is a belief that we are all daughters of Hagar and Sarah. Their commonalities, despite the conflicts they experience, can create a foundation of reconciliation through faith. This chapter will provide a historical account of Hagar and Sarah's story to inspire us all toward Imani.

Hagar in the Jewish Tradition

In the Tanakh or Hebrew Bible, Jews interpret the Hagar and Sarah story as one of conflict and coexistence. Two women vie for position in the household of Abraham and in the eyes of God.[7] Sarah, as the Israelite matriarch, is portrayed as superior to Hagar who is her servant and Abraham's Egyptian concubine. Hagar is considered inferior in ethnicity, and in social and marital status compared to Sarah, but her fertility gives her superiority. "Sarah's superiority is restored when God intervenes on Sarah's behalf so that Sarah conceives and then bears Abraham's son Isaac."[8] The relationship between the two women is volatile and ultimately Sarah banishes Hagar and Ishmael. Hagar survives and finds her son a wife.

For Jewish interpreters, the biblical story of Hagar and Sarah contrasts a choice between two central values: devotion for their Jewish descendants, and concern for the weak, which is part of biblical and Jewish tradition.[9] Postbiblical sources, from the second century BCE through the second century CE, provide many texts that tell the story of Hagar and Sarah. For example, Josephus Flavius, the first-century Jewish historian, in his text titled *Jewish Antiquities,* favors Sarah, and portrays Hagar as "immature, ignorant, and misguided."[10] He emphasizes a positive image of Sarah and Abraham and chooses to ignore the moral issues that are innate in the biblical scriptures.[11] Philo of Alexandria, a postbiblical author, "interprets the Bible as an elaborate allegory for the soul's journey to wisdom."[12] He emphasizes Sarah's superiority as he explains that the name Hagar means "sojourning" while Sarah means "virtue."[13]

Other Jewish interpreters emphasize that Hagar is no ordinary slave woman. She is the daughter of Pharaoh. Likewise, some feminist and womanist writers and commentators view the two women's relationships from different perspectives.[14] For example, "African American readers have lovingly claimed Hagar as their own, made her a foremother, taken pride in her struggle, formed spiritual churches in her name, and led the way in creative appropriations of her story."[15]

Hagar in the Muslim Tradition

In the Muslim tradition the story of Hagar, Sarah, Abraham, Ishmael, and Isaac is of "central significance as written in the Qur'an and in the hadith (oral traditions of the Prophet Muhammad)."[16] It is a source of strength and courage, hope and faith for Muslims. Muslims believe that the Qu'ran is the word of God, revealed through the Archangel Gabriel to the Prophet Muhammad.[17] The Qu'ran does not mention either Hagar or Sarah by name, but it does make reference to Abraham's wife (Surah 51). The "Qu'ran pays little attention to the wives of Abraham even though they are critical for . . . relationships of Muslims to Jews and Christians."[18]

Although the story of "Hagar is not mentioned in the Quran it is given considerable detail in *Sahih Al-Bukhari*."[19] Hagar is portrayed as "a woman of exceptional faith, love, fortitude, resolution, and strength of character. Despite the challenges in Hagar's relationship with Sarah she surrenders to God's will and chooses to dwell in the desert to which God had directed her, making a home and community out of an unknown land and people."[20] Hagar raises her son, Ishmael, with a deep awareness of God's presence. Abraham's leaving Hagar and Ishmael in the desert are interpreted not as wanting to please Sarah, but as "show[ing] that he believes in order to fulfill prophetic mission of Building the Sacred House of God (which Muslims believe to be the first House of God at Mecca) it was necessary to leave a part of his family in the uninhabited, uncultivated land."[21] Abraham believes that this land will become populated and fruitful and that Hagar and Ishmael will find sustenance and love in their new environment.[22] Repeatedly the Quran depicts Ishmael as prophet, an apostle, and a just man over humankind (e.g., Surah 6:86; 19:54; 38:48).[23] Respect for Hagar continued to her death. Tradition says that she was buried in Mecca near the Ka'bah, where later Ishmael was buried. To this day their tombs belong to the holy places of Islam and Hagar is honored as the matriarch of monotheism.[24]

Hagar in the Christian Tradition

In the scripture unique to Christians, the New Testament, there is division and disparity between Hagar and Sarah.[25] At the same time, Scripture emphasizes unity, that we are all children of Abraham and Sarah.

> So also Abraham "believed God, and it was credited to him as righteousness." Understand, then, that those who have faith are children of Abraham. Scripture foresaw that God would justify the Gentiles by faith, and announced the gospel in advance to Abraham: "All nations will be blessed through you." So those who rely on faith are blessed along with Abraham, the man of faith. (Gal 3:6-9 NIV)

Christian commentaries use exegetical strategies similar to rabbinic interpretation and by the middle of the third century "Hagar" and "Sarah" become codes for "synagogue" and "church."[26] For example, "Origen of Alexandria (d. 251) cites God's promise to Abraham that his descendants will be as numerous as the stars (Gen. 15:5)."[27] More than a century later, John Chrysostom of Antioch (d. 407) denounces Jews as "Christ killers."[28] Augustine of Hippo (d. 430) argues that the Jews descend from Hagar while Christians are the "seed of Abraham."[29] These early church fathers continued to foster division between the children of Hagar and Sarah. I wonder if early women of the church would have supported these perspectives.

Imani (Faith) in Action

Beyond historical divisions, sometimes stoked by religion, as humans we long for harmony with a community of people. We desire to be connected with others who have similar interests and beliefs and to make a positive difference in the lives of others. Faith leads us to invite, welcome, receive, and care for others, to nurture dialogue and take action together. It describes a genuine love for others who are diverse, because we share values. It is openness, adaptability, and willingness to change behaviors in order to accommodate the greater needs of the whole community, especially those who suffer.[30] Hagar and Sarah, despite their conflict, symbolize radical empathy. Radical means being significantly distinct from the usual practice, surpassing expectations, going beyond tradition, and by faith enabling people to thrive. In the context of education, Hagar and Sarah's empathy can inspire us all to radically support children and families despite the diversity of places we live, faith we inherit, or traditions we hold. Here's an example from the Missouri United Methodist Annual Conference's Open Hearts, Open Books initiative as one pathway out of poverty.[31]

Stories have power. Reading paves a path to a broader and brighter world—unlocking imaginations, expanding possibilities and improving the probability of a successful future. Partnered with local schools, Missouri United Methodist Churches are invited to grow and deepen their existing school-church partnerships through the intentional giving of books.

Give a book. Expand a story. Build a relationship.

It's about relationships.

As a church we recognize that relationships are incredibly powerful. We don't want to give outside of a relationship; we want schools, teachers and students to know that we're working in partnership with them. We're on their team, doing life with them and being concerned about their whole selves. They are more than their needs.

Local churches participating in the 100,000 books challenge should have an already established church-school partnership. Don't have one?

Learn how you can build one.

It isn't transactional.

Churches—after they have spent time cultivating their current partnership—will work with their partner school to identify the best way to connect books with students. The expectation is that a church volunteer has personally connected with the student receiving the book and that the book chosen is specific to the student receiving it.

You may want to provide books for the entire school. That is wonderful! If you have a book fair, read-a-thon or other literacy-focused endeavor with your local school partner, we celebrate you! In order for a book to count towards [sic] your pledge, the church must have a relationship with the school, the teacher and the student. You aren't just giving away books; you are connecting students that you know to books.

Because the church volunteer has connected with the student, they will pick a book that is age-appropriate and honors the diversity of students' backgrounds, languages, abilities, perspectives and interests. Pick a book the student can see themselves in! Volunteers will read the book with the student or discuss it with them. It's more than a book, it's a connection.[32]

Faith, *Imani*, is a belief with all our heart in God, in people, in parents, in teachers, in leaders, and in the righteousness and victory of our struggle. The struggles we encounter are personal, communal, and systemic. They are found at home, in organizations, and woven through school systems, church systems, and even the highest levels of governments. Cultivating faith, Imani, through prayer, study, worship, and serving others provides a pathway to inner peace, conflict resolution, and systemic justice. We must not give up, but instead keep the faith.

Main Points to Remember

- Historically, faith has given people the ability to trust God (or a higher power) and one another in the midst of adversity. There is a deep knowing that trust is built through dialogue and action across time, geography, cultures, and experience. Trusting then can enable endurance and liberation to overcome violence and heal underlying causes of conflict.

- Beyond historical divisions, sometimes stoked by religion, as humans we long for harmony with a community of people. We desire to be connected with others who have similar interests and beliefs and to make a positive difference in the lives of others.

- "Stories have power. Reading paves a path to a broader and brighter world—unlocking imaginations, expanding possibilities and improving the probability of a successful future. Partnered with local schools, churches can grow and deepen their existing school-church partnerships through the intentional giving of books. Give a book. Expand a story. Build a relationship."

- Cultivating faith, Imani, through prayer, study, worship, and serving others provides a pathway to inner peace, conflict resolution, and systemic justice. We must not give up, but instead keep the faith.

Questions for Discussion and Action

As you cultivate faith, Imani, consider the following questions to discuss with your team, neighbors, or group of concerned citizens.

How do you intentionally stretch out of your comfort zone, engage people, and offer yourself to actions that you would never have done if not for your faith in God and others?

What would it take to push beyond your normal circle of relationships that routinely define your commitments? How would it change the lives of the people and communities who are served, as well as the lives of those who serve?

Intentional community development can be nurtured through intercultural learning in community. How can you connect with people of different cultures and faiths to build relationships and nurture peace?

Conclusion

A Call to Advocacy

I was a good student throughout school. I worked hard to get good grades because I loved the feeling of achievement. I always wanted to be the smartest in the class. I carefully read the directions to each assignment, completed each part methodically, and checked the answers twice. I was eager to get A's and be affirmed for my intellect. Even today I love writing lists and checking items off at the end of the day.

In college I was invigorated by math and poured myself into a business curriculum. Yet, I was even more intrigued by marketing and learning how people make decisions. I read my assignments three times, took notes, and could regurgitate the business philosophies my professors taught. I treasured my study time and was exceptionally committed to being a great student. I graduated magna cum laude, the top 10 percent of my class.

Surrounded by a supportive community of family and friends, education changed my life and afforded me the opportunity to work as a marketing manager in corporate America.

Yet, after toiling for twelve years and being promoted on average every two years, I questioned whether the promotions, titles, rewards, power, and opportunities were worth the cost. My feelings of restlessness were a sign for me to pay attention. This was the beginning of learning to trust my own gut and the messages deep within my soul.

One day during this restless season I received an invitation to visit Saint Paul School of Theology. Out of nowhere, it seemed I was interested enough to visit the school. That day I went home with the resolve to take a deeper journey into my faith and to pursue a master of divinity degree. Sometime later I embraced my unusual vocation as a minister. I would have never predicted this would be the course of my life.

All this happened more than ten years ago. During seminary I slowly learned to trust my own thoughts and feelings and to first look inside myself for wisdom. I began to write, not just regurgitate what others said. I discovered my own voice. Here's an excerpt from my early writing journey in seminary.

> Writing is my work. I am called to hone this craft to somehow build the kingdom, share wisdom, and carry on stories so that future generations will benefit from what God says to me. I let go of all my fears . . . what if it's not good . . . what if no one reads it . . . it does not matter . . . I will still write. I will learn the craft, practice the craft, and share it with others. Writing is liberation! Writing is like the very air I breathe. Listening is part of what makes this possible. I will listen with my heart. I will appreciate others and what they have to offer knowing that we are all children of God. I thank you for my sisters and foremothers that have walked this path before me and for those who now sow into me. I am, therefore I write. I am, therefore I listen with my heart. I am, therefore I sow forward in all that I do. I do the hard stuff and celebrate along the way. Will it be easy? No. Will it be worth it? Absolutely.

Communicating is a gift. Whether you write, speak, dance, sing, draw, or make music, your innate talent and strengths have the power to positively impact the world when combined with others.

The beauty of the American democracy is that all citizens have the right to vote and speak. We all are an essential part of conversations and decisions about what occurs in our nation. Through advocacy and organizing we can influence decision makers and the future of America. When we meet and talk with elected officials and other decision makers, when we write letters, send emails, and make phone calls, we have the power to educate them about our lived experiences. We have the power to encourage them to understand our needs and desires as parents and community members. We thus can hold elected officials accountable for incorporating diverse viewpoints into their decisions, to support the common good.

Advocacy is how ordinary citizens transform themselves into powerful, vocal education champions. We are more powerful than we realize when we use our collective people power. In fact, a study conducted by the Congressional Management Foundation discovered constituent visits to the Washington, DC, office (97 percent) and to the district/state office (94 percent) have "some" or "a lot" of influence on an undecided member of Congress.[1] Policymakers themselves shared: "Every policy issue goes through three stages: education, activation and implementation. Congress is a stimulus response institution."[2] Conversations with family, friends, and colleagues, even on social media, can become tools of citizenship. In these conversations we can listen to another person's point of view, and we can explain and defend our own. These conversations can form the seeds for larger, more public advocacy, becoming op-eds and letters to the editor to our local newspapers, where a larger sphere of people can "hear" and consider our point of view. This is just one expression of advocacy, a simple way for individuals or small groups of people to use their voices together.

Education is discussed and practiced every day in local communities, state houses, and on Capitol Hill. If we want policy decisions to reflect what's best for all students and families in our communities, we must proactively add our voices. We must assert ourselves, initiating and participating in the work of advocacy. Those who are most impacted by disparities in education and opportunity must be centered in these conversations and this work.

Questions for Discussion and Action

What have you read in these pages that lights a spark within you?

What idea is ruminating?

Where do you need to increase your knowledge or deepen your understanding?

Who are the people and organizations—school, church, and civic—you are curious enough to contact, to begin a conversation about working together?

We end where this book began, with a dream that faith, education, inspiration, and lived experience can lead us forward as a community.

I believe solutions to the world's biggest challenges can flow through prayer, writing, dialogue, and collective action.

I believe individuals and groups of people can and will decide to come together to change education and provide more opportunity in our country.

I believe the seven foundational principles of Kwanzaa offer a powerful, purposeful framework for our collaboration.

I believe we can learn from historical and current examples—and actually bring about—positive change.

If you have read this book, you probably share at least some of these convictions.

Peace be with you, as you do justice, love mercy, and walk humbly.

Partnership Actions You Can Take Now

You've absorbed the ideas and information offered in this book, learned about the principles of Kwanzaa, read the stories of educational inequity, and glimpsed the transformation that happens when opportunity is for all. Now what?

Use the following lists as the starting point for your work as an individual, a leader, or a group. First, work through the preceding chapters, and take the time to consider the main points and questions. Record your questions, ideas, and any conclusions you draw from that reading and discussion. Does this lead you in any particular direction? Do you feel a call or a tug on your heart toward one principle or one type of need?

Next, read through the list below. It includes specific actions you can take individually or as a group. It is organized by the Kwanzaa principles and into categories—Education, Service, and Systems Change. Choose one step or action. Develop a plan and follow it through to completion. Come back to the principles, the questions, and the list below regularly to develop, build, and sustain your efforts. You will make a difference.

1. Partnering in Unity: Public Education

Education: Talk with school administrators and teachers with the objective of becoming better informed about the needs of the public schools in your communities and in the country. Only through adequate information can we defend public education and the democratic heritage which it supports. All children have the right to a quality education that utilizes the best educational techniques and honors their humanity.

Service: Volunteer your time to provide support for under supported schools and students in need. Support programs that strengthen and spread education in society, whether it is a school lunch program, an adult literacy program, a book donation program, a local tutoring center, or some other program with direct impact.

Systems Change: Advocate at the state and local level for adequate public school funding and equitable distribution of state funds. Support efforts to end unjust educational disparities between rich and poor communities. Push for quality universal preschool education for all children. Champion public education as a basic human right.

2. Partnering for Self-Determination: Substance Abuse, Alcohol, and Tobacco

Education: Learn about the root causes and manifestations of substance abuse, including alcohol and tobacco. Contact your local school and community leaders to find out what is happening in your community to prevent substance use, abuse and addiction among youth. Ask how you can help.

Service: Partner with others in your church and community who share a passion for substance abuse prevention and recovery. Create or support a recovery ministry (Alcholics Anonymous, Narcotics Anonymous, and Celebrate Recovery) in your community.

Systems Change: Urge your local legislative bodies and health-care systems to implement measures to help meet the special needs of those disproportionately affected by substance abuse. These measures include eliminating advertising and promotion of nicotine products and alcoholic beverages, and developing better health hazard warning statements concerning their use.

3. Partnering by Collective Work and Responsibility: Civic Engagement

Education: Learn about civics, voting and local elections in your area. Look for programs that help more people vote, such as nonpartisan voter registration efforts. Look for groups working to increase people's engagement in electoral processes. Consider how you might work with these groups.

Service: Offer programs that ensure youth gain knowledge and experience through school- based civic education, service learning, and youth development. Participate in the U.S. Census and encourage others to also participate.

Systems Change: Meet with your local elected officials to discuss initiatives that impact democracy, such as campaign finance, re-districting, and election processes. Urge them to ensure safe, accessible and secure elections.

4. Partnering through Cooperative Economics: Food Systems

Education: Learn about the root causes and manifestations of food injustice, sustainability and sovereignty. Food systems that are ecologically sustainable, locally oriented, and equitably distributed provide access to healthy nourishment and clean drinking water.

Service: Discuss with your church and community leadership ideas to reduce food waste and to support farm workers. Connect with your neighborhood in support of local farmer's markets or community gardens. Provide or support local nutritional initiatives, especially when schools are not in session.

Systems Change: Support workers throughout the food chain—from those who harvest our food to those who process, transport, and serve it. Join with food workers as they campaign for better wages and working conditions. Advocate for policies that support healthy and sustainable agriculture, humane treatment of animals, and access to affordable, nutritious food.

5. Partnering for Purpose: Human Worth

Education: Learn about the root causes and manifestations of genderism, racism, ethnocentrism, tribalism, and any ideology or social practice based on false and misleading beliefs that one group of human beings is superior to other groups of human beings. Ask trusted, neutral experts for recommendations of books, articles, webinars, and documentary films.

Service: Create or support leadership opportunities for students (especially girls and ethnic minorities) so they learn about their gifts and talents and begin to practice how they will use their abilities to become authentic, powerful leaders in their church, school and community.

Systems Change: Challenge unjust systems of power and access. Work for equal and equitable opportunities in education and training, employment and promotion. Work for equal and equitable access to public accommodations and housing, credit, loans, capital, and insurance. Work for equal and equitable access to free, safe voting in every election. Work for equal and equitable access to positions of leadership and power in all elements of our life together and to full participation in the church and society.

6. Partnering with Creativity: Climate Change

Education: Recognize the inherent worth of all creation, and celebrate earth's abundance and diversity, along with the entirety of the cosmos. Learn how your lifestyle and the institutions you are a part of are connected to the climate crisis. Use an online carbon footprint calculator to measure your emissions and take steps to reduce your carbon footprint. Celebrate God's creation and discuss the climate crisis with others in your community.

Service: Adopt sustainable habits and practices, including refraining from overconsumption, repurposing and recycling materials, avoiding products that pollute or otherwise harm the environment, and reducing the carbon footprints of individuals and families by reducing overall reliance on fossil fuels for heat, transportation and other goods.

Systems Change: Contact your elected officials and advocate for policies and practices that build a clean energy future and support frontline communities struggling to survive in a changing climate. Support cooperative efforts aimed at redressing the ecological harms humans have wreaked on a global scale.

7. Partnering in Faith: Poverty and Income Inequality

Education: Learn about the root causes and manifestations of poverty and income inequality. Learn about local tax and spending decisions.

Service: Provide essential needs such as food, clothing, short term rent/utility assistance, and temporary shelter to families in need.

Systems Change: Contact your elected officials to remind them that budgets are moral documents and should uplift the common good, support the poor and vulnerable and build peace in community and among nations. Advocate for just policies to require transparency and limit extreme interest rates and fees.

Suggested Resources

https://www.umcjustice.org/

https://www.umc.org/en/how-we-serve/advocating-for
-justice/racial-justice/united-against-racism

About the Author

The year was 1965. The determined and committed young college student was a history major; a member of the Historical Society, Interfraternity Council, S.N.E.A., Young Democrats, Student Council; president of Kappa Alpha Psi; a student mentor; and featured in Who's Who. In meetings of the Young Democrats, debates were held, films shown, and speakers presented to stimulate interest in democracy.[1] One of the most notable accomplishments of these young students at Northeast Missouri State Teachers College, led by a Methodist campus minister in Kirksville, Missouri, was to integrate the lunch counter of a local hotel. They were inspired by the civil rights protests that began in 1960, "when young African American students staged a sit-in at a segregated Woolworth's lunch counter in Greensboro, North Carolina, and refused to leave after being denied service. The sit-in movement soon spread to college towns throughout the South. Though many of the protesters were arrested for trespassing, disorderly conduct, or disturbing the peace, their actions made an immediate and lasting impact, forcing Woolworth's and other establishments to change their segregationist policies."[2] Likewise, the actions of this group of college students and faith leaders led to the integration of restaurants and hotels, thus paving the way for equal access to public accommodations for all. That determined and committed history student was Louis Virdure. He went on to become a high school and college history teacher, attorneyof-law, and track coach. As my father, he inspires me to advocate for justice and unity for all.

The year was 1965. She migrated to St. Louis from Philadelphia, Mississippi, with her family to find better opportunities and a better life. Her family, like "six million [other] African-Americans[,] left the South from 1915–1970."[3] They left to escape the limitations and the threats of Jim Crow. They left to get better jobs. They left for the promise of more options for housing, health care, and schools. They left to find better lives.[4]

She is the great granddaughter of John "Jack" Johnson, born between 1820–1822. Jack was enslaved in North Carolina, Alabama, Louisiana, and Mississippi. Oral history suggests unconfirmed locations of Tennessee, Virginia, and the Caribbean Islands. Jack brought his family together in Kemper County, Mississippi, to flourish amid racial strife after the Civil War. Jack had twenty children. Strength of family, hard work, and education created the backbone of this family.

She is the granddaughter of Georgia "Carline" Johnson, born August 1, 1875, in Kellis Store, Kemper County, Mississippi. She was called "mama." She is the daughter of Verna M. Perryman and Irvin Culberson. Verna, affectionately called "mother," lived to the age of ninety-six. This is my mother, Mildred Louise Culberson Virdure. As a mom, college graduate, and businesswoman, she inspires me to nurture family, connect with community, and maintain hope.

> When we look at our ancestors, we see varying degrees of color. A beautiful array in shades of the brown earth and alabaster.
>
> Labeled; black, colored, yellow, negro, mulatto, passing white and the litany of other names that disrespect and strip away humanism. Names that reflect a past slave culture of property.
>
> Those unfamiliar with the way of the South or too young to recall the one drop rule can't quite grasp how the "white" ancestors were still considered black and subjected to the same segregation laws. Why those of color still suffered injustices after the emancipation proclamation.[5]

I am the daughter of African American parents united in love for fifty-one years of marriage despite their differences in geography, culture, and experiences from the North and South. What binds them and us is a *practice of solidarity and embracing connectedness in family and community.* This is the spirit in which I live, love, and seek unity.

I am a child of hip-hop culture. Born in 1972, I remember hearing my first rap album in 1980. One early morning before school my father surprised my brother and me with the new album by the Sugarhill Gang featuring "Rapper's Delight." They sang, "Hip, hop, you don't stop the rockin'. To the bang-bang boogie, . . ." I grew up with hip-hop in the 1990s as I sang and danced to new school hip-hop and R & B artists such as LL Cool J, Queen Latifa, Run DMC, and eventually the Fugees and Lauryn Hill. These artists not only entertained us but they also had a profound impact on the shaping of our identities. For young Black girls and boys, rap music had a greater impact on our consciousness than any sermon, writing assignment, or public service announcement. "Rap is the rock 'n' roll of the day," Bill Adler said in *Time* magazine in 1990. "Rock 'n' roll was about attitude, rebellion, a big beat, sex and, sometimes, social comment. If that's what you're looking for now, you're going to find it here."[6] We found rap music, break dancing, fly clothes, and the overall attitude captivating and empowering. It gave voice and beat to a piece of our culture.

The ingenuity of hip-hop artists and culture across the past four decades is undeniable. At its best, hip-hop continues to inspire radical creativity and honor the uniqueness revolutionized by Black America. Even in its sometimes-offensive form, it speaks of truth in the language of the people. This is the essence of Kuumba as truth telling, community rooted, captivating and empowering.

Notes

Introduction

1. Lee's Summit R-7 School District, March 13, 2020, "LSR7 Health Update 3/13/2020: Novel Coronavirus (COVID-19)," https://lsr7.org/news/lsr7-health-update-novel-coronavirus-covid-19/.

2. A. H. Maslow, "Classics in the History of Psychology—A. H. Maslow (1943) A . . . ," https://psychclassics.yorku.ca/Maslow/motivation.htm, accessed February 4, 2021.

3. Leah Asmelash, "Kwanzaa: The Seven Principles of Kwanzaa," December 26, 2019, https://www.cnn.com/2019/12/26/us/kwanzaa-principles-trnd/index.html, accessed February 4, 2021.

4. "Kwanzaa—What Is It?" *Akwansosem* 3, no. 2 (March 1990), https://www.africa.upenn.edu/K-12/Kwanzaa_What_16661.html, accessed February 4, 2021.

5. Dirk J. Louw, "Ubuntu: An African Assessment of the Religious Other," in Philosophy in Africa, http://www.bu.edu/wcp/Papers/Afri/AfriLouw.htm. Accessed December 9, 2020.

6. Louw, "Ubuntu: An African Assessment of the Religious Other."

7. Louw, "Ubuntu: An African Assessment of the Religious Other."

8. Michael Bungay Stanier, *The Coaching Habit: Say Less, Ask More and Change the Way You Lead Forever* (Toronto: Box of Crayons, 2016), Kindle edition, 24–28.

1. Public Education in the US

1. "BLS History," https://www.bls.org/apps/pages/index.jsp?uREC _ID=206116&type=d, accessed February 4, 2021.

2. Walter Herbert Small, *Early New England Schools* (Charleston, SC: Nabu Press, 2013), 91.

3. Small, *Early New England Schools,* 91.

4. "Historical Timeline of Public Education in the US," Race Forward, https://www.raceforward.org/research/reports/historical-timeline -public-education-us, accessed February 4, 2021.

5. Oregon State University, "Section II-American Education," https:// oregonstate.edu/instruct/ed416/ae1.html, accessed February 4, 2021.

6. Library of Congress, "America at Work, America at Leisure: Motion Pictures from 1894 to 1915," https://www.loc.gov/collections/america-at -work-and-leisure-1894-to-1915/articles-and-essays/america-at-school/, accessed February 4, 2021.

7. "11 Facts About the History of Education in America," American Board, July 1, 2015, https://www.americanboard.org/blog/11-facts -about-the-history-of-education-in-america/.

8. "11 Facts About the History of Education in America."

9. "John Dewey: My Pedagogical Creed," June 21, 2013, https:// infed.org/mobi/john-dewey-my-pedagogical-creed/.

10. W. E. B. Du Bois, "The Talented Tenth," https://books.apple .com/us/book/the-talented-tenth/id514813017.

11. "How Much Wealthier Are White School Districts Than Nonwhite Ones? $23 Billion, Report Says," February 27, 2019, https://www.nytimes.com/2019/02/27/education/school-districts-funding-white-minorities.html.

12. "11 Facts About the History of Education in America," American Board, July 1, 2015, https://www.americanboard.org/blog/11-facts-about-the-history-of-education-in-america/.

13. Grady Wilburn, Brian Cramer, and Ebony Walton, "The Great Divergence: Growing Disparities between the Nation's Highest and Lowest Achievers in NAEP Mathematics and Reading between 2009 and 2019," https://nces.ed.gov/nationsreportcard/blog/mathematics_reading_2019.aspx, accessed May 18, 2021.

14. W. E. B. Du Bois, "The Talented Tenth."

2. Partnering in Unity: Umoja

1. United Nations, Social Inclusion, https://www.un.org/development/desa/socialperspectiveondevelopment/issues/social-integration.html, accessed May 18, 2021.

2. "Honoring the History of Hickman's Mill," *Martin City Telegraph*, December 13, 2020, https://martincitytelegraph.com/2020/12/13/honoring-the-history-of-hickmans-mill/.

3. "Honoring the History of Hickman's Mill."

4. Aaron Tyler Rife, "Shifting Identities in South Kansas City: Hickman Mills's Transformation from a Suburban to Urban School District," (PhD diss., University of Kansas, 2014), https://kuscholarworks.ku.edu/bitstream/handle/1808/15154/Rife_ku_0099D_13466_DATA_1.pdf?sequence=1, accessed January 15, 2021.

5. Hickman Mills C-1 School District, "Hickman Mills C-1 School District Overview," https://www.hickmanmills.org/domain/34, accessed February 4, 2021.

6. Jami Parkison, "The Journey to Our Future: The History of Hickman Mills C-1 School District, 1902–2002" (Kansas City, MO: Hickman Mills C-1 School District, 2002), 69, located in Rife, "Shifting Identities in South Kansas City."

7. Rife, "Shifting Identities in South Kansas City," 85–86.

8. Rife, "Shifting Identities in South Kansas City," 131.

9. Rife, "Shifting Identities in South Kansas City," 158.

10. Rife, "Shifting Identities in South Kansas City," iv.

11. "How to Find a Person of Peace Even When You Don't Know Anybody," October 9, 2018, https://freshexpressionsus.org/2018/10/09/how-to-find-a-person-of-peace-even-when-you-dont-know-anybody/.

12. Racial Equality Institute, "The Groundwater Approach," https://www.prnewswire.com/news-releases/racial-equity-institute-releases-groundwater-approach-whitepaper-to-educate-organizations-about-systemic-racism-300823007.html, accessed May 26, 2021.

13. Racial Equality Institute, "The Groundwater Approach."

14. Isabel Wilkerson, *Caste: The Origins of Our Discontents* (New York: Random House, 2020), 18–19.

15. Wilkerson, *Caste*, 18–19.

16. United Believers Community Church, "#WeChurchDifferent," https://believeandbelong.life/, accessed February 4, 2021.

17. "As Homicide Numbers Soar, Clergy Partner with Kansas City Police to Reduce Violence," August 11, 2020, https://www.kansascity.com /news/local/crime/article244872797.html, accessed February 4, 2021.

3. Partnering for Self-Determination: Kujichagulia

1. Olaudah Equiano, *The Interesting Narrative of the Life of Olaudah Equiano: Written by Himself*, ed. with an introduction by Robert J. Allison (Boston and New York: Bedford Books of St. Martin's Press, 1995), 2.

2. Equiano, *Interesting Narrative of the Life of Olaudah Equiano*, 1.

3. Vincent Carretta, *Equiano, the African: Biography of a Self-Made Man* (Athens: University of Georgia Press, 2005), xi.

4. Equiano, *Interesting Narrative of the Life of Olaudah Equiano*, 199.

5. "Olaudah Equiano," *Encyclopedia Britannica*, March 27, 2021, https://www.britannica.com/biography/Olaudah-Equiano, accessed May 19, 2021.

6. "Democracy Means People Power, Literally (with Eric Liu)," Baratunde, August 21, 2020, https://www.baratunde.com/how-to-citizen -episodes/02-people-power.

7. Dan Yarnell, "The Spirit says 'yes': exploring the essence of being church in the 21st century." *Evangel*, vol. 26, no. 1 (Spring 2008): 9–14.

8. J. Gordon Melton, *A Will to Choose: The Origins of African American Methodism* (United Kingdom: Rowman & Littlefield, 2007), foreword.

9. Matthew Weyer and Jorge E. Casares, "Pre-Kindergarten-Third Grade Literacy," December 17, 2019, https://www.ncsl.org/research/education /pre-kindergarten-third-grade-literacy.aspx, accessed February 4, 2021.

10. "Fourth Grade Reading Achievement Levels in the United States," Kids Count Data Center, https://datacenter.kidscount.org/data/tables/5116 -fourth-grade-reading-achievement-levels, accessed February 4, 2021.

11. Annie E. Casey Foundation, "EARLY WARNING! Why Reading by the End of Third Grade Matters," http://www.thefundsdp.org /uploads/AECF-Early_Warning_Full_Report-2010.pdf, accessed February 4, 2021.

12. "Find the Best Public High Schools," *U.S. News and World Report*, https://www.usnews.com/education/best-high-schools, accessed February 4, 2021.

13. Emily A. Vogels, "59% of U.S. Parents with Lower Incomes Say Their Child May Face Digital Obstacles in Schoolwork," Fact Tank, September 10, 2020, https://www.pewresearch.org/fact-tank/2020/09/10/59 -of-u-s-parents-with-lower-incomes-say-their-child-may-face-digital -obstacles-in-schoolwork/.

14. John A. Powell, Stephen Menendian, and Wendy Ake, "Targeted Universalism: Policy & Practice," Haas Institute, May 2020, https:// belonging.berkeley.edu/sites/default/files/targeted_universalism_primer .pdf, accessed February 4, 2021.

15. Powell, Menendian, and Ake, "Targeted Universalism," 16.

16. "United Methodist Revised Social Principles," https://www.umc justice.org/documents/124, accessed February 4, 2021.

4. Partnering by Collective Work and Responsibility: Ujima

1. Carol S. Dweck, *Mindset* (New York: Ballantine, 2007).

2. Carol Dweck, "The Power of Believing that You Can Improve," TED Talk, December 17, 2014, https://www.ted.com/talks/carol

_dweck_the_power_of_believing_that_you_can_improve/transcript, accessed February 4, 2021.

3. Renaissance, "Growth Mindset," https://www.renaissance.com /edwords/growth-mindset/, accessed February 4, 2021.

4. Dweck, "The Power of Believing that You Can Improve."

5. Dweck, "The Power of Believing that You Can Improve."

6. Valerie J. Calderon and Daniela Yu, "8 Things You Need to Know about Students," Gallup, May 25, 2017, https://news.gallup.com/opinion /gallup/211028/eight-things-need-know-students.aspx, accessed February 4, 2021.

7. "Gallup Student Poll National Report—America's Promise Alliance," https://www.americaspromise.org/sites/default/files/d8/legacy /bodyfiles/GSP%20National%20Report.pdf, accessed May 26, 2021.

8. Isabel Wilkerson, *Caste: The Origins of Our Discontents* (New York: Random House, 2020), 18.

9. Ewing Marion Kauffman Foundation, "It's Time to Rethink Education," https://realworldlearning.kauffman.org/wp-content/uploads/sites /11/2020/06/real_world_learning_infographic.pdf, accessed January 18, 2021.

10. National Center for Education Statistics, quoted in Ewing Marion Kauffman Foundation, "It's Time to Rethink Education."

11. "The Mentoring Effect-ERIC-US Department of Education," https://files.eric.ed.gov/fulltext/ED558065.pdf, accessed May 26, 2021.

12. Valerie J. Calderon, "How to Spot and Develop Extreme Teaching Talent," Gallup, April 14, 2014, https://news.gallup.com/opinion /gallup/173618/spot-develop-extreme-teaching-talent.aspx, accessed February 4, 2021.

13. Mary Reckmeyer, *Strengths Based Parenting: Developing Your Children's Innate Talents* (Washington, DC: Gallup Press, 2016), Kindle edition.

14. Reckmeyer, *Strengths Based Parenting*.

15. Christina Theokas and Reid Saaris, "Finding America's Missing AP and IB Students," The Education Trust, June 2013, https://sites.ed.gov /underservedyouth/files/2017/01/MS3-Lead-Higher-Initiative-Finding -Americas-Missing-AP-and-IB-Students.pdf, accessed February 4, 2021.

16. Theokas and Saaris, "Finding America's Missing AP and IB Students."

17. "The Economic Impact of the Achievement Gap in America's Schools," McKinsey & Company, April 2009, https://dropout prevention.org/wp-content/uploads/2015/07/ACHIEVEMENT_GAP _REPORT_20090512.pdf, accessed February 4, 2021.

18. Theokas and Saaris, "Finding America's Missing AP and IB Students."

19. Theokas and Saaris, "Finding America's Missing AP and IB Students."

20. Theokas and Saaris, "Finding America's Missing AP and IB Students."

21. Theokas and Saaris, "Finding America's Missing AP and IB Students."

22. Schott Foundation for Public Education, "Opportunity Gap Talking Points," http://schottfoundation.org/issues/opportunity-gap/talking -points, accessed February 2, 2021.

23. Lee-Ann Stephens, "A Phenomenological Study of the Students Who Were Actively Engaged in the High Achievement Program at a Suburban High School" (PhD diss, Bethel University, 2014), https://www.forestofthe

rain.net/uploads/3/5/8/2/3582998/a_phenomenological_study_of_the
_students_who_were_actively_engaged_in_the_high_achievement
_program_at_a_suburban_high_school.pdf, accessed February 2, 2021.

5. Partnering through Cooperative Economics: Ujamaa

1. "CCD Philosophy: Christian Community Development Association," https://ccda.org/about/philosophy/, accessed May 20, 2021.

2. "About Cicero, Illinois," https://thetownofcicero.com/about-cicero-illinois/, accessed February 4, 2021.

3. "North Lawndale History," https://static1.squarespace.com/static/5ce5a0a707d84d0001f09e17/t/5da4a7226d3f39358b772b0f/1571071778389/North+Lawndale+History.pdf, accessed February 4, 2021.

4. "North Lawndale History."

5. Lawndale Christian Community Church, http://www.lawndalechurch.org/, "About Our Lead Pastor," accessed February 4, 2021.

6. Lawndale Christian Development Corporation, https://lcdc.net/, accessed February 4, 2021.

7. "Christian Community Development Association," https://ccda.org/, accessed February 4, 2021.

8. *Making Neighborhoods Whole: A Handbook for Christian Community Development*, https://www.amazon.com/Making-Neighborhoods-Whole-Christian-Development/dp/0830837566, accessed February 4, 2021.

9. Wayne Gordon and John M. Perkins, *Do All Lives Matter?: The Issues We Can No Longer Ignore and the Solutions We All Long For* (Grand Rapids: Baker, 2017), Kindle edition.

10. Gordon and Perkins, *Do All Lives Matter?*

11. "Communities Creating Opportunity," https://cco.org/, accessed February 1, 2021.

12. "Re:Dream: Elliott Clark," PBS, March 30, 2016, https://www.pbs.org/video/redream-elliot-clark/.

13. "CCD Philosophy: Christian Community Development Association," https://ccda.org/about/philosophy/, accessed May 20, 2021.

6. Partnering for Purpose: Nia

1. Dictionary.com, s.v. "purpose," https://www.dictionary.com/browse/purpose, accessed February 4, 2021.

2. My Daily Kwanzaa, s.v. "Purpose (Nia)," https://mydailykwanzaa.wordpress.com/purpose-nia/, accessed February 4, 2021.

3. Della Lamb Community Services, "Educational & Support Services," https://www.dellalamb.org/services/, accessed February 4, 2021.

4. My Daily Kwanzaa, "Purpose –".

5. Della Lamb Community Services, "Education & Support Services," https://www.dellalamb.org/services/, accessed February 4, 2021.

6. Della Lamb Community Services, "Education & Support Services," https://www.dellalamb.org/services/youth-services/, accessed February 4, 2021.

7. Della Lamb Community Services, "Refugee Resettlement," https://www.dellalamb.org/services/, accessed April 23, 2021.

8. *The Missouri Methodists Magazine*, Missouri Conference of The UMC, https://www.moumethodist.org/magazine, accessed February 4, 2021.

9. Faith in Action Newsletter, https://live-faith-in-action.pantheonsite.io/wp-content/uploads/2019/11/FIA-Clergy-Letter.pdf, accessed February 1, 2021.

10. Robby Berman, "The Story of 'Lift Every Voice and Sing,'" February 19, 2020, https://bigthink.com/politics-current-affairs/lift-every-voice, accessed February 4, 2021.

11. My Daily Kwanzaa, s.v. "Purpose (Nia)," https://mydailykwanzaa.wordpress.com/purpose-nia/, accessed February 4, 2021.

12. "19th Amendment to the U.S. Constitution: Women's Right to Vote (1920)," https://www.ourdocuments.gov/doc.php?doc=63, accessed February 4, 2021.

13. Connor S. Kenaston, "From Rib to Robe: Women's Ordination in The United Methodist Church," *Methodist History* 53, no. 3 (April 2015), accessed February 4, 2021.

14. Cheryl Townsend Gilkes, *If It Wasn't for the Women . . . : Black Women's Experience and Womanist Culture in Church and Community* (Maryknoll, NY: Orbis, 2000).

15. Barbara Ransby, *Ella Baker and the Black Freedom Movement: A Radical Democratic Vision* (Chapel Hill and London: University of North Carolina Press, 2003), 4.

16. Ransby, *Ella Baker and the Black Freedom Movement*, 188.

17. Dictionary.com, s.v. "purpose," https://www.dictionary.com /browse/purpose, accessed February 4, 2021.

18. My Daily Kwanzaa, s.v. "Purpose (Nia)," https://mydailykwanzaa .wordpress.com/purpose-nia/, accessed February 4, 2021.

19. Wan-Lae Cheng, Cameron Davis, Andrea Dua et al., "Lessons from the Past on How to Revive the US Economy after COVID-19," June 18, 2020, McKinsey & Company, https://www.mckinsey.com/industries /public-sector/our-insights/lessons-from-the-past-on-how-to-revive-the -us-economy-after-covid-19?cid=other-eml-alt-mip-mck&hlkid=72412e 3d41ac4318afe872ea0e04b0f3&hctky=11623188&hdpid=26e515d9-c6 7a-44af-9528-98725b757bce.

7. Partnering with Creativity: Kuumba

1. Clifton Taulbert and Gary Schoeniger, *Who Owns the Ice House?: Eight Life Lessons from an Unlikely Entrepreneur* (Washington, DC: ELI Press, 2010), Kindle edition.

2. Taulbert and Schoeniger, *Who Owns the Ice House.*

3. Angela Duckworth, *Grit: The Power of Passion and Perseverance* (New York: Scribner, 2016).

4. Vauadi Vibila, "Marginalization," in *Dictionary of Feminist Theologies*, ed. Letty M. Russell and J. Shannon Clarkson (Louisville: Westminster John Knox Press, 1996), 170.

5. Michael L. Cook, "Yield Not to Temptation: Confronting the Financial Challenges of the Black Family," in *Multidimensional Ministry for Today's Black Family*, ed. Johnny B. Hill (Valley Forge, PA: Judson Press, 2007), 76.

6. "Andre M. Perry," Brookings Institution, https://www.brookings.edu/experts/andre-m-perry/, accessed January 31, 2021.

7. Andre M. Perry, "Know Your Price: Valuing Black Lives and Property in America's Black Cities" (Washington, DC: Brookings Institution Press, 2020), "Introduction: Assets of Home."

8. Chris Haslam, *Revised Common Lectionary Commentary*, http://montreal.anglican.org/comments/archive/cpr03l.shtml, accessed April 26, 2010.

9. Wilkerson, *Caste*, 17.

10. "What Is Radical Empathy?" Camp Stomping Ground, February 16, 2017, https://campstompingground.org/blog/2017/2/16/what-is-radical-empathy, accessed January 31, 2021.

11. Anne Gregory and Katherine R. Evans, "The Starts and Stumbles of Restorative Justice in Education: Where Do We Go from Here?" January 14, 2020, https://nepc.colorado.edu/publication/restorative-justice, accessed February 4, 2021.

12. CrossMarks Christian Resources, "Luke 4.14-21: 3rd Sunday after the Epiphany-Year C," http://www.crossmarks.com/brian/luke4x14.htm, accessed February 4, 2021.

13. Marvin A. McMickle, *Preaching to the Black Middle Class: Words of Challenge, Words of Hope* (Valley Forge, PA: Judson Press, 2000), 9.

14. Citizens UK, "Staff," https://www.citizensuk.org/staff, accessed January 31, 2021.

15. Matthew Bolton, *How to Resist: Turn Protest to Power*, https://www.amazon.com/How-Resist-Turn-Protest-Power/dp/1408892723, accessed January 31, 2021.

16. Bolton, *How to Resist*, 3–4.

17. Duckworth, *Grit*.

18. Nancy Callahan, "Freedom Quilting Bee," *Encyclopedia of Alabama*, August 8, 2008, http://encyclopediaofalabama.org/article/h-1628, accessed January 31, 2021.

8. Partnering in Faith: Imani

1. Melissa Macaya, Meg Wagner, Veronica Rocha, and Mike Hayes, "Democrats take control of the Senate," January 6, 2021, https://www .cnn.com/politics/live-news/georgia-senate-runoff-election-results/index .html, accessed February 4, 2021.

2. Julia Jacobo, "This Is What Trump Told Supporters before Many Stormed Capitol Hill," January 7, 2021, https://abcnews.go.com/Politics /trump-told-supporters-stormed-capitol-hill/story?id=75110558, accessed February 4, 2021.

3. Morgan Winsor, Ivan Pereira, and William Mansell, "4 Dead after US Capitol Breached by Pro-Trump Mob during 'Failed Insurrection,'" ABC News, January 7, 2021, https://abcnews.go.com/Politics/capitol -breached-protesters/story?id=75081629, accessed February 4, 2021.

4. Centers for Disease Control and Prevention, "COVID Data Tracker," January 28, 2021, https://covid.cdc.gov/covid-data-tracker/, accessed May 26, 2021.

5. "Dr. Martin Luther King Jr.," Smithsonian Institution, https:// www.si.edu/spotlight/mlk?page=4&iframe=true, accessed February 4, 2021.

6. Phyllis Trible and Letty M. Russell, "Unto the Thousandth Generation," in *Hagar, Sarah, and Their Children: Jewish, Christian, and Muslim Perspectives*, ed. Phyllis Trible and Letty M. Russell (Louisville: Westminster John Knox, 2006), 1.

7. Adele Reinhartz and Miriam-Simma Walfish, "Conflict and Co-existence in Jewish Interpretation," in *Hagar, Sarah, and Their Children*, 101.

8. Reinhartz and Walfish, "Conflict and Coexistence in Jewish Interpretation," 101.

9. Reinhartz and Walfish, "Conflict and Coexistence in Jewish Interpretation," 102.

10. Reinhartz and Walfish, "Conflict and Coexistence in Jewish Interpretation," 103.

11. Reinhartz and Walfish, "Conflict and Coexistence in Jewish Interpretation," 103.

12. Reinhartz and Walfish, "Conflict and Coexistence in Jewish Interpretation," 104.

13. Reinhartz and Walfish, "Conflict and Coexistence in Jewish Interpretation," 104.

14. Reinhartz and Walfish, "Conflict and Coexistence in Jewish Interpretation," 115.

15. Reinhartz and Walfish, "Conflict and Coexistence in Jewish Interpretation," 120.

16. Riffat Hassan, "Islamic Hagar and Her Family," in *Hagar, Sarah, and Their Children*, 149.

17. Hassan, "Islamic Hagar and Her Family," 150.

18. Trible and Russell, "Unto the Thousandth Generation," 6.

19. Hassan, "Islamic Hagar and Her Family," 153.

20. Hassan, "Islamic Hagar and Her Family," 154.

21. Hassan, "Islamic Hagar and Her Family," 153.

22. Hassan, "Islamic Hagar and Her Family," 153.

23. Trible and Russell, "Unto the Thousandth Generation," 7.

24. Trible and Russell, "Unto the Thousandth Generation," 10.

25. Trible and Russell, "Unto the Thousandth Generation," 3.

26. Trible and Russell, "Unto the Thousandth Generation," 8.

27. Trible and Russell, "Unto the Thousandth Generation," 8.

28. Trible and Russell, "Unto the Thousandth Generation," 9.

29. Trible and Russell, "Unto the Thousandth Generation," 9.

30. Robert Schnase, *Five Practices of Fruitful Congregations* Extract, http://robertschnase.com/wp-content/uploads/2015/10/Guide_Curran 08_BURRKSBT.pdf, accessed May 26, 2021.

31. "Open Hearts, Open Books," https://openheartsopenbooks.org/, accessed April 24, 2021.

32. "Open Hearts, Open Books," https://openheartsopenbooks.org /get-involved/, accessed April 24, 2021.

Conclusion: A Call to Advocacy

1. "Perceptions of Citizen Advocacy on Capitol Hill," Congressional Management Foundation, https://www.congressfoundation.org /projects/communicating-with-congress/perceptions-of-citizen-advocacy -on-capitol-hill, accessed February 2, 2021.

2. "Perceptions of Citizen Advocacy on Capitol Hill."

About the Author

1. Truman State University, "Student Government Resolution 117.0015," March 4, 2018, http://senate.truman.edu/files/2018/03/A -Resolution-for-Reconditioning-the-Library-Pit-117.0015.pdf, accessed February 4, 2021.

2. "Greensboro Sit-In," History.com, February 4, 2010, https://www .history.com/topics/black-history/the-greensboro-sit-in.

3. Sally J. Altman, "Migration in Hope of a Better Life," St. Louis Public Radio, February 9, 2011, https://news.stlpublicradio.org /government-politics-issues/2011-02-09/migration-in-hope-of-a-better -life.

4. Altman, "Migration in Hope of a Better Life."

5. "The Johnson Family of Kemper County Mississippi: Murder and Mayhem," https://johnsonfamilyofkempercounty.com/murder-and -mayhem/, accessed February 4, 2021.

6. Janice C. Simpson, "Yo! Rap Gets on the Map," *Time*, February 5, 1990, https://web.archive.org/web/20071113221827/https://www.time .com/time/magazine/article/0,9171,969341,00.html.

Made in the USA
Monee, IL
05 March 2024

54482707R00075